Eric Reader and Pamela Woods

Introducing the Novel

An Approach to Literature for GCSE

Bell & Hyman

Published by BELL & HYMAN
An imprint of UNWIN HYMAN LIMITED
Denmark House
37/39 Queen Elizabeth Street
London SE1 2QB

British Library Cataloguing in Publication Data
Reader, Eric
    Introducing the novel : an approach to
    literature for GCSE.
    1. Fiction
    I. Title   II. Woods, Pamela
    808.3   PN3365

    ISBN 0-7135-2752-8

Designed by Buzzard Book Design

Illustrated by Peter Edwards and Julie Sailing

Typeset by Tradespools Ltd., Frome, Somerset

Printed in Great Britain

Contents

Acknowledgements

For permission to reproduce copyright material, the authors and publishers are indebted to the following: the author's estate and the Hogarth Press for an extract from *Tiger in the Smoke* by Margery Allingham; Blackie & Son Ltd for an extract from *Joby* by Stan Barstow, and three extracts from *Conrad's War* by Andrew Davies; The Bodley Head for extracts from *Sumitra's Story* by Rukshana Smith and *Wild Boy* by Joan Tate; Jonathan Cape Ltd for extracts from *The Wolves of Willoughby Chase* by Joan Aiken, *Danny the Champion of the World* by Roald Dahl and *Run for your Life* by David Line; Chatto & Windus and the Hogarth Press for an extract from *Cider with Rosie* by Laurie Lee; J M Dent & Sons Ltd for an extract from *Summer of the Zeppelin* by Elsie McCutcheon; Andre Deutsch for two extracts from *My Mate Shofiq* by Jan Needle; Victor Gollancz Ltd for extracts from *A Handful of Thieves* by Nina Bawden, *Z for Zachariah* and *Mrs Frisby and the Rats of NIMH* by Robert C. O'Brien; William Heinemann Ltd for an extract from *The Pearl* by John Steinbeck; Hodder & Stoughton Ltd for an extract from *Frankenstein's Aunt* by Allan Rune Pettersson; Michael Joseph Ltd for three extracts from *A Kestrel for a Knave* by Barry Hines; Macmillan Ltd for an extract from *The Diddakoi* by Rumer Godden; Methuen Children's Books Ltd for an extract from *I Am David* by Ann Holm; Oxford University Press for extracts from *The Black Lamp* by Peter Carter (1973), *The Dark Behind the Curtain* by Gillian Cross (1982), *Warrior Scarlet* by Rosemary Sutcliff (1958) and *Tom's Midnight Garden* by A. Philippa Pearce (1958); Pan Books Ltd for an extract from *The Restaurant at the End of the Universe* by Douglas Adams (1980); two extracts from *Smith* by Leon Garfield (Longman Young Books, 1967), copyright © Leon Garfield, 1967, reproduced by permission of Penguin Books Ltd; Routledge & Kegan Paul Ltd for two extracts from *Grandad with Snails* by Michael Baldwin; the author for two extracts from *A Pair of Jesus-Boots* by Sylvia Sherry, © Sylvia Sherry 1969; John Rowe Townsend for three extracts from his novel *Gumble's Yard*.

The following photograph sources are also acknowledged; Fay Godwin's Photo Files, p.42; Sally & Richard Greenhill, p.11.

The publishers have made every effort to trace owners of copyright material, but in some cases this has not proved possible. The publishers would be glad to hear from any copyright owners not acknowledged here.

1 *Novels and authors*

What is a novel?

That question is not only the most obvious, but also the most difficult to answer. That's why it's taken us a whole book to explain what we think constitutes a novel. You have probably been told countless times that if you're not sure what a word means then look it up in a dictionary. We decided to take our own advice with the word 'novel':

> 'Fictitious prose narrative of volume length portraying characters and actions representative of real life in continuous plot.'

Now you understand perfectly, don't you? No? Well, you're right – it doesn't help that much really. Which is why, during the course of this book, we will try to answer some of your questions. We will also attempt to introduce you to different types of novels and see how they are put together.

You may ask yourself why you should read a book instead of, say, watching television. The answer is, quite simply – for enjoyment, the sort of enjoyment that television can never provide.

Another logical question you may ask yourself is why you should study the novel when you could spend the time reading another book.

Obviously we think it is important to study the novel or we wouldn't have written this textbook. There are many reasons why we study the novel: greater understanding of a particular book, knowledge and understanding of the characters, interpretation of plot, recognition of style and setting; but again, hopefully, a clearer understanding of the novel will lead to a higher level of enjoyment for the reader. The writer wishes to entertain, as well as, in some cases, instruct.

Talking about books

The aim of the following questions is to get you thinking and talking about books.

1 Are you reading a book at the moment? What is the book's title? What is the author's name? Is it your own book or is it a school book?

2 Are you a regular reader or do you have to be persuaded by your teachers?

3 Do you often read for pleasure? What sort of things do you read? Comics? Magazines? Novels?

4 How much time do you spend reading as opposed to other activities? Working with a partner, or in a small group, attempt to find out the reading habits of your form.

5 Discuss with a partner how your own reading habits have changed during the past few years. Can you remember any favourite books from your early childhood?

6 Do you ever buy books for yourself? Do you ever buy a book as a present? Discuss your answers with a partner.

7 What sort of book would you like to be given as a present? Discuss your choice with a partner.

8 Working in a small group, improvise a television or radio programme where members of the panel are discussing their favourite books.

Here are some notes that may prove useful.

Author
The author of a book is the person who wrote it.

Title
The title is the name of the book.

Publisher
The publisher is the person or company that produces and sells the book on behalf of the author.

The blurb
The blurb is the publisher's description of a book, usually found on the inside flap of the jacket, or – if a paperback – on the back cover.

Front flap

Title, author, publisher

Front cover

Back cover

Back flap

Two London teenagers are faced with seemingly insurmountable difficulties as they discover that their friendship has deepened into something that must overcome cultural differences and family opposition if it is to survive.

Here is a story with a strong sense of 'here and now'. "Strangers on Saturdays" will appeal to anyone who has had to battle with school, teachers, parents and friends before finding a solution to their problems.

£4.95

Strangers on Saturdays

John Bowden

Strangers on Saturdays   John Bowden   ⒷⒷ

"One of the most compelling stories I have read in a long time."
J. HAWTHORN, LONDON PRESS

"The scope and sensitivity of this work make it a unique achievement."
BOOK REVIEW WEEKLY

"A most remarkable novel"
STANDARD NEWS

Photo

John Bowden was born in Stapleford on July 12th 1937. Educated at the local grammar school, he went on to study English and History at the University of London.

"Strangers on Saturdays" is John Bowden's first novel written for the teenage fiction market. It is shortly to be serialised for children's television.

Blurb, price

Design, picture, title, author

Spine, publisher's logo

Design, quotes from reviews

Author, photograph, relevant biographical details, list of any previous books

The spine

The spine is the backbone of the book and it holds the pages and cover together.

The title page

The title page shows the name of the author, title, illustrator, editor, series and publisher.

Preface or introduction

This usually gives details of the book, its themes and purpose. It is sometimes written by the author if he wishes to give any relevant information to help the reader to understand the book.

Chapter headings

Not all authors give their chapters headings, while some books are not actually divided into chapters at all. The majority of books do have chapter headings, however, and many authors view them as being an important aspect of their work.

We hope you liked our dust jacket for the 'novel' *Strangers on Saturdays* on page 7. It is, of course, only an example.

You won't find a copy of *Strangers on Saturdays* in any library or bookshop. What you *will* find are hundreds and thousands of *real* books written by *real* people. John Bowden *isn't* a real person.

We 'invented' him – just as a real author 'invents' his novels and characters. If you've ever struggled to 'invent' a story for an English essay or composition, you may have wondered how a novelist manages.

Well, let's imagine we *could* interview John Bowden. What questions would we ask him? More importantly, what answers would we get? . . .

INTERVIEWER: John. The obvious question. Why write?

JOHN: It's a challenge – a way of sharing things with other people. It's a means of communicating with people, just as, say, painting or music are.

INTERVIEWER: So why novels? Why not short stories or poetry?

JOHN: I find that in a novel you can spread yourself. There are no limitations on space or time. All experience is open to you.

INTERVIEWER: You say 'all experience'. Does that mean a novel can be about anything?

JOHN: Yes, I think so. It can be a ghost story, a love story, a story set in the past or in outer space. It can be funny, sad, terrifying – any number of things. Whatever, in fact, the author wants to share with his audience.

INTERVIEWER: I find the word 'audience' interesting. Does it mean you regard the novel as a form of entertainment?

JOHN: Yes – but a good novel does more than just entertain. From the reader's point of view, it should open a door to his understanding – make him more aware of the world than he was before.

INTERVIEWER: But surely you wouldn't expect everyone who reads one of your books suddenly to feel this greater awareness?

JOHN: Of course not, but that's the beauty of a good novel. It's a work of art, which means it can have as many levels as there are people who read it. Remember, a good novel usually remains with the reader as part of himself. He will recall bits of it now and again, enjoy the memory of it, and in that way continue to gain pleasure from it.

INTERVIEWER: You make the job of the novelist sound a very responsible one. Tell me, do you think anyone can write a good novel?

JOHN: Probably not. It needs a lot of patience and, above all, a powerful imagination. So powerful, in fact, that when you see something in your own mind it can seem more real than things outside your mind. It's the ability to sit in a room in, say, London or Manchester and believe that you are somewhere else – a different place, with different people, often in a different time scale completely.

INTERVIEWER: And is that how you begin work on a new novel – by imagining yourself somewhere else?

JOHN: It depends. There are no hard and fast rules. In my case, when I make up a story there has to be a spark to begin with – a central idea that more often than not seems to come quite by chance. If it has the right 'feel' to it, then the plot will begin to form in my head almost without my having to think about it. Then the real work begins.

INTERVIEWER: Devising your characters, you mean?

JOHN: Yes, that and working out the details of the plot. I usually find myself writing the opening scenes over and over again, trying to work out exactly where the story should start.

INTERVIEWER: I've heard it said that a good title will often sell a book. Where do your titles come from, John?

JOHN: Just occasionally, a title will come like magic, even before I write a word of the book. But more often than not, I find titles for my books after they are written. Then it takes me weeks and weeks to make up my mind and I have to ask everyone round me for suggestions. After that, it's all down to the publishers . . .

Activities

The following questions can be answered orally, or with a written response, or used as a starting point for drama work.

1 Working in a small group, choose one person who is going to take on the role of a well-known author. Now improvise a situation where the other members of the group interview the author. Remember to ensure that the author you decide upon is well known by all the members of the group.

2 Prepare a talk about a book you have read recently. Give a brief outline of the story and say whether you enjoyed the book or not. Remember to give reasons for your opinions.

3 Do you think that you need to be an accurate observer of people and situations to make a good writer? Give reasons for your answer. Try to think of several qualities that a writer needs, and say why you think they are important.

4 Keep a notebook for twenty-four hours. Ensure that you record as accurately as possible all the events that happen during that time. Give the notebook to a friend and try to relate, in as much detail as possible, all the events that you recorded. Did you miss anything important?

5 What are your opinions of serialised books on television?

6 Outline the advantages that books have over the television or radio. Can you think of any disadvantages that books may have?

7 Think of a book you have enjoyed and say why you think it should be serialised either for radio or television. What difficulties do you think would be encountered?

8 Working in a small group, imagine that John Bowden has arrived at your school to give a talk concerning the pleasures of reading and writing. One of the group must take on the role of John Bowden and the others will ask suitable questions.

Let's look at publicity

Turn back to the dust jacket of *Strangers on Saturdays*. The artist has interpreted the novel in a particular manner. The design of a book's cover is very important and can be a great help in the sale of the novel.

Why do you think this is so? When you choose a book from the library or a bookshop, to what extent are you influenced by the book's cover or illustrations? Why do you think that publishers often put a photograph from a film or television series on the cover of a book?

Discuss your answers with your teacher or a partner.

Activity

Using the notes and the plan you were given earlier in the chapter, make up a new title for the book you are reading at the moment and design a new dust jacket. Remember that you will need to include a suitable blurb and some notes about the author.

Extended activities

1 You may have to do some research for this one, but nothing too difficult. Look in a local paper or one of the nationals and see if they have a list of bestsellers. If not you could try your local bookshop. Working with a partner, compile a list of the top ten bestselling paperbacks for this month. Then compile a list of the top ten general books for this month. Why do you think the Bible or Shakespeare never appear on any bestseller list?

2 Working with a partner, conduct a survey on how well your school or local library is used by members of your form. You could include interviews, questionnaires, written accounts or any other relevant information.

3 Design a poster to encourage pupils to use the library more frequently. You might decide to link your advertising campaign to National Book Week. Perhaps you could also include a competition to find a suitable slogan for the week.

4 Write an illustrated guide to your school library to help either a first-year pupil or a new member of staff to get to know the library.

5 What do you think libraries of the future will look like? Do you think we will still have books? What sort of books, if any, do you think you would find in a library in the year 2500? Perhaps you could include some sketches or diagrams to illustrate your answer.

6 Some people are in the fortunate position of having a classroom library. Put yourself in the position of a teacher who is just about to start such a library. What books do you think you would include? What qualities are essential for a good library regardless of size?

7 Look at the quotes on the next page. Choose four quotes with which you agree and say why. Then choose four quotes (if possible) with which you disagree. Give reasons for your choice.

8 Allow yourself about fifteen minutes and just jot down what you think a good book should contain. What makes you want to continue reading a book? What qualities must it have?

9 When you have finished question eight, discuss your opinions with a partner. Have you both written down the same opinions? Has either of you missed out anything the other feels is essential?

10 Compile a list of the five books that you would take to a desert island. When you have completed your list try to write a paragraph about each book explaining why you have chosen it.
　Now compare your list with that of a partner. Are there any books that you both have on your list? Make a 'Top Ten' list for the whole form.

2 Beginnings and endings

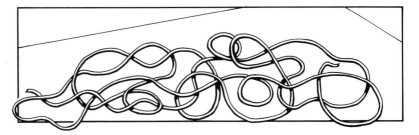

Let's start with an activity. Find the beginning of the above piece of string. Right, now find the end. What do you mean, it's too difficult? How do you know which is which? Well, we're afraid that's your problem because we were only asked to set the activity! Fortunately, the beginnings and endings of novels are not quite so confusing.

Consider the following:

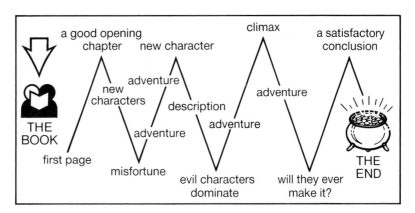

The journey or the way through a book

Openings

If the first few pages of a book are dull, boring or confusing, the reader may not bother to read any more. The first rule of the novelist, therefore, is to catch your attention at the beginning of the novel. Having caught your attention, the book must be interesting enough to hang on to it! If you think about it, the author has to introduce you to characters, and situations – or both. He also needs to make the reader feel there is a good story on the way. It is important that a balance is kept between action, dialogue, and characters. In other words, the start of a book must grab your attention, but not confuse you by presenting too many characters or too much action.

This is why many people think that the beginning of a novel is much more important than the ending.

Look at the following beginnings from *The Dark Behind the Curtain* and *The Diddakoi*. You may find one is more interesting than the other. Discuss with a partner the opening you found the most effective. Try to describe why you found it effective.

The heavy red curtain swirled outwards and settled into long folds. From behind it shuffled a stooped figure, alert and menacing, his fingers gripping something long and straight which glittered as he stropped it restlessly against his other hand.

'They all come' – the voice was low and gloating – 'rich and poor, old and young, they all need the barber.' His feet inched forward over the boards. 'I sit them in my chair and I lather 'em up to the nose, watching their silly faces in the mirror, dreaming of fine dinners and fancy women. No eyes for the barber as comes creeping, creeping . . .'

'Then, all of a sudden—' the figure jerked upright and in his right hand something bright flashed once, slicing murderously down. '—I *cuts* 'em! From ear to ear! And the blood drips down their shirts and puddles on the floor.'

The left hand traced the slump of a head, the slow sliding of a body. 'And then' – briskly – 'into the cellar with 'em and off to be chopped up and rolled in pie crust.'

His laugh shivered through the silence.

Jackus, leaning against the door at the back of the Hall, shuddered involuntarily. Somehow, he had not expected anything so good. As the laugh died away, there was a hush. For a full minute, nobody spoke.

Then fat Ann Ridley broke the tension with a nervous giggle: 'That was *beastly*, Marshall!'

'That was *tremendous*, Marshall!' said another voice. Miss Lampeter jumped to her feet, her fair hair swinging, and clapped her hands. 'That's just what I wanted.'

From *The Dark Behind the Curtain* by Gillian Cross

'If anyone,' said the teacher, Mrs Blount, in the classroom, 'anyone,' and her eyes looked sternly along the lines of tables filled with boys and girls, 'teases or bullies or jeers at Kizzy Lovell, they will answer for it to me.'

Twenty-eight pairs of eyes looked back at Mrs Blount blandly and innocently: 'As if we would,' they seemed to say. The twenty-ninth pair, Kizzy's, looked down at her table; she had a curious burning in her ears.

'To me,' said Mrs Blount. 'We shall not have such behaviour in this school.' But they would; silent and small, Kizzy knew that.

'Kizzy must be short for something,' Mrs Blount had asked her. 'What is your real name, dear?'

'Kizzy.'

Mrs Blount had touched a sore spot: in Kizzy's family, as in some gypsy clans, a child is given three names: a secret one whispered by its mother the moment it is born and, when it is grown, whispered again into the child's ear; a private or 'wagon' name which is used only by its own people, and a third open name by which it's known to the world. Kizzy seemed only to have one, but that was because she was what they called her, a 'diddakoi', not all gypsy. 'We don't say gypsies now. We say travellers,' Mrs Blount told the children. Kizzy's father, pure Rom, had married an Irish girl, but Kizzy looked gypsy to the children and they were half fascinated, half repelled by her brownness and the little gold rings in her ears – none of the other girls had golden ear rings.

From *The Diddakoi* by Rumer Godden

Activity

Choose several books from your school or local library. Read at least the first four pages, but if possible the first chapter. Make brief notes on your reaction to each novel. Which novel would you continue to read and why? You might wish to record your answers on a chart like the one shown below. You might also decide to report back to the rest of your form on the best two openings you found.

Title of book	Author	Read the book? (Yes/No)	Reasons for answer

Direct openings

A Handful of Thieves by Nina Bawden actually tells the reader what the rest of the book is going to be about.

> This is the story of how we became a gang of thieves. My sister Jinny says I shouldn't start like this, giving away the story in the first sentence, but I think she's wrong. If you're writing a book, you've got to make sure the right sort of people read it, haven't you? Otherwise it's not fair to them or to you. So I'm starting off by saying this is a book about thieves and robbers so that no one who would rather read about fairies or magic or talking animals need bother to go any further. It's about me and my friends and how we turned thieves and brought a criminal to justice.

From *A Handful of Thieves* by Nina Bawden

Activity

What do you think of this opening paragraph? Do you think it's a good idea for the main character to speak to the reader directly? Would you now want to read the rest of the novel? Why?

Here is another example of the main character speaking directly to the reader, but in a very different manner.

> May 20th
> I am afraid.
> Someone is coming.
> That is, I think someone is coming, though I am not sure, and I pray that I am wrong. I went into the church and prayed all this morning. I sprinkled water in front of the altar, and put some flowers on it, violets and dogwood.
> But there is smoke. For three days there has been smoke, not like the time before. That time last year, it rose in a great cloud a long way away, and stayed in the sky for two weeks. A forest fire in the dead woods, and then it rained and the smoke stopped. But this time it is a thin column, like a pole, not very high.

From *Z for Zachariah* by Robert C. O'Brien

The main character talks directly to the reader but also creates an atmosphere of suspense and mystery. The author has used both techniques here. Ask yourself the same questions as before concerning this opening. Discuss your response with a partner.

Descriptive openings

Some novels begin with a description of a character given by another character or by the author himself.

> Billy Griffiths limped down the last flight of stairs, one hand clutching the bannister for support. In the harsh neon light, his face was screwed up with effort and anxiety. It was anxiety mostly, for Billy, crippled by polio when he was eight, was accustomed to putting a bit of effort into getting around.

From *A Pair of Jesus-Boots* by Sylvia Sherry

Activity

Look at the novel you are reading at the moment. How does it begin? Do you think the beginning is interesting or exciting? Would you have started the book in a different way?

Analyse your beginnings

Here is the chart we use when we analyse the beginnings of novels.

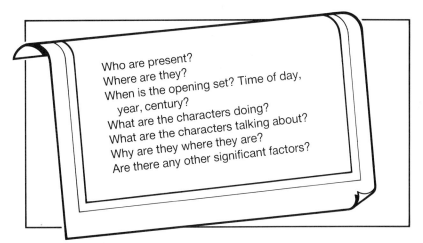

Who are present?
Where are they?
When is the opening set? Time of day, year, century?
What are the characters doing?
What are the characters talking about?
Why are they where they are?
Are there any other significant factors?

Activity

Using the above question chart analyse the following openings to *The Black Lamp* by Peter Carter and *Frankenstein's Aunt* by Allan Rune Pettersson. Discuss your answers with a partner.

I was born in the village of Helmshaw in the Vale of Rossendale, in Lancashire, in the year 1803, when our country was at war with the armies of the French Republic. A soldier's scarlet coat was then a sign of glory and 'King and Country' was all the Patriots' cry, but still there were those, like my father, who asked, 'Whose King and whose country?' and who thought that the 'Ça Ira' was as good a tune as any they had heard.

My father's name was George Cregg. He was named for a king, but myself he called Daniel, after that hero of the Hebrews who went into a lions' den for his beliefs. My mother died giving birth to my sister, Emma. I was but five years old then and so I scarcely remember her. She is buried under a slab of millstone in Hashingden churchyard and, when I can, I go there and place a sprig of flowers on her grave.

Because of my mother's death my father had to be both mother and father to me and I, in turn, had to be both brother and mother to Emma. Had my father been in any other trade he would have had to marry again, but he was a hand-weaver and they, you must know, do their work at home, and so our father could earn our bread and watch over us as well.

From *The Black Lamp* by Peter Carter

The old lady leant back and lit a cigar. She was beginning to get thoroughly fed up with this journey. If only her secretary had come with her, as had been decided from the start, but he was in bed at home with yet another cold. 'He ought to see a specialist about all those colds,' she thought irritably. And then the railway company had the nerve to call this *first* class, which she thought was nothing but a mockery to an old person. The seats were dreadfully saggy and the lighting quite beyond the pale, one single light bulb in a bell-shaped pink shade spreading a dim trembling light over the compartment. It was almost impossible even to think of reading. Several times she had tried to make some kind of sense out of the notes her nephew had left behind, but it was impossible in this light. The boy was certainly good at making a mess of things, anyhow, that much she had managed to fathom.

From *Frankenstein's Aunt* by Allen Rune Pettersson

Implied and stated information

When an author gives any information he does, in fact, give two sorts of information, stated and implied. Look again at the extract from *Frankenstein's Aunt* and decide what is stated and what is implied. You might decide to set your work out as shown below.

Title of book:	Author:
Information stated	**Information implied**
old lady lit a cigar	*very unusual old lady*

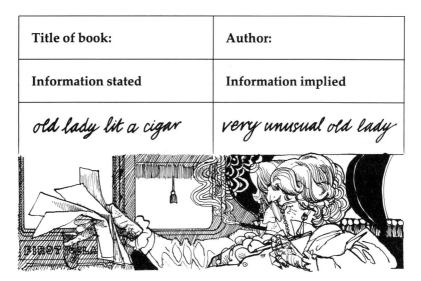

Using the same chart, look at the opening chapter of the novel you are reading at the moment. Of course, you can use the chart to analyse any section of your book to decide on the type of information you are being given.

Endings

If openings are important, then so are endings. It used to be the accepted form to complete a novel by telling the reader what happened to all the major characters after the novel had finished. The modern novel finishes with the end of the story. We no longer expect a novel to tell us every detail, although we do perhaps sometimes wonder what the next events would be if the author was to write a sequel.

There are as many different ways of opening and concluding a novel as there are authors to write them. However, it is possible to arrange both beginnings and endings into some sort of order.

Look carefully at the following chart and if possible add any others you have encountered.

Beginnings	Endings
Action beginnings	Back to normal
Description of place	What's happened to everyone
Dialogue	since
Evoke a mood or create	Unravelling a complex plot
atmosphere	Surprise endings
Description of character	Endings with a twist
Formula, e.g. Once upon a	Unfinished endings
time . . .	Anti-climax endings
Shock/surprise	Open endings
Combinations of methods	

Activity

Consider the final paragraphs of the last novel you read. How did the book finish? Were you satisfied with the conclusion? Were you surprised at how the book ended?

Of course, we all have our own preferences when it comes to endings. We like a book that has all the loose ends tied up in a satisfactory manner. Gordon Taylor in his book *Creative English* does not agree, however:

An Irishman, on being told that the first coach and the last were usually the ones to suffer most severely in train crashes, was inspired to suggest that the obvious remedy was to run trains without such coaches. That Irishman must have been a remote ancestor of mine, for I maintain that books should have no last chapters.

Activity

In small groups, discuss the endings of various books you have read recently. What are the thoughts of the group? Do people have preferences or does it depend on the type of novel being read? Why do you think so many books have sequels? Present the findings of your group in the form of an oral report to the other groups.

Look back to the list given above. Read the following passage and try to say what type of ending *My Mate Shofiq* has. Discuss your answer with a partner.

'It's me dad I'm feared for,' Shofiq said. His voice was odd; there was no tone to it, no expression. 'Maybe that Burke does believe what he's doing's right. Maybe he does think it's for our own good. But what will me dad do without me? What can he do? I've got to look after him, to help him. I'm the one that keeps that family going. What's going to happen to me dad?'

Bernard couldn't follow too well, but it seemed right. Wendy and Shofiq were staring at each other. They seemed to understand each other right well.

Wendy said: 'I'll tell them that, Shofiq. I'll do my best. I'll tell them that.' She rattled the front door one last time.

Shofiq said sadly: 'And d'you think they'll listen, Wendy? Do you?'

She made a funny little face, and took hold of Bernard's hand. With her other hand, the right one, she took hold of Shofiq's.

'Come on,' she said. 'Let's go and face the music.'

Shofiq looked at her, his big eyes bright and grave.

'Are you holding me to stop me running away?' he said quietly.

'Don't be so daft,' said Wendy. 'You're Bernard's mate. I'm holding you because I like you. All right?'

A small smile appeared on Shofiq's face.

'Yes,' he said. 'All right.'

They went to face the music.

From *My Mate Shofiq* by Jan Needle

Activity

Consider a book you have read recently and answer the following questions:

(a) How was the plot drawn to a conclusion?
(b) What were the reactions of the main characters?
(c) What is the effect of the final sentence?
(d) How final is the final chapter?
(e) Did you expect the conclusion or were you surprised?
(f) Were you satisfied with the ending? Give reasons for your answer.
(g) Would you change the ending in any way? Give reasons for your answer.
(h) Would you like to read a sequel to this book? Give reasons for your answer.

Dramatic endings

A book that has a particularly dramatic ending is *I Am David*.

A few yards would take him to the door, and yet David thought he would never get there. His legs could carry him no farther and he was on the point of collapsing. He had thought for some time that perhaps if the woman who lived there would tell him what to do, and where to go, he would be able to manage, but now he knew he couldn't. If his happiest dreams came true, he could go on living: if not this was the end.

French was the language he spoke best. David picked up his bundle, walked to the door and rang the bell. When the woman opened it, he knew she was the woman in the photograph, the woman whose eyes had seen so much and yet could smile.

Then David said in French, 'Madame, I'm David. I'm . . .'

He could say no more. The woman looked into his face and said clearly and distinctly, 'David . . . My son David . . .'

From *I Am David* by Ann Holm

Activity

At this point we require you to be perfectly honest. If you know, or have read, the book *I Am David*, then you must attempt B. If you do not know the book then you may attempt either A or B, or both.

Briefly write down what you think led up to that final section of the book. What sort of adventures do you think David had and what type of people did he meet?

Script the scene between David and his mother. You may introduce any other characters if you wish. In small groups act out one incident from the book.

Ending or beginning?

To end this chapter that has been concerned with beginnings and endings, here is a beginning and ending to a book that you may make of what you will.

The beginning

It was a fine spring day, not warm but with a sort of hazy sunshine, . . . Summer was coming, the blades of grass were showing between the stone setts, and soon the weeds would blossom on the empty sites. The days were getting longer. Next week perhaps we would be playing cricket after school. There was a dog in Mimosa Row that I was getting very friendly with. I was going to make a soap-box car for my cousin Harold. Life was full of interesting things to do.

We walked three abreast, with Sandra in the middle. And as we turned into Orchid Grove I felt happy and burst out singing.

'Hark at him!' said Sandra. 'Not a care in the world.'

'Poor old Kevin!' said Dick, with mock sympathy. 'He's got a pain. Where does it hurt, Kevin?'

'I'll hurt *you* in a minute!' I said.

'Oh yes? You and who else?'

'Do you think I couldn't?'

'Yes, I do think you couldn't.'

'Well, I'll show you.' And we started a friendly scuffle, the kind that happens a dozen times a day.

The ending

It was a fine spring day, not warm but with a sort of hazy sunshine. Summer was coming, the blades of grass were showing between the stone setts, and soon the weeds would blossom on the empty sites. The days were getting longer. Next week perhaps we would be playing cricket after school. There was a dog in Mimosa Row that I was getting very friendly with. I was going to make a soap-box car for Harold. Life was full of interesting things to do.

We walked three abreast, with Sandra in the middle. And as we turned the corner into our own street I felt happy and burst out singing.

'Hark at him!' said Sandra. 'Not a care in the world.'

'Where does it hurt, Kevin?' asked Dick with mock sympathy.

'I'll hurt *you* in a minute!' I said.

And we started a friendly scuffle, the kind that happens a dozen times a day.

From *Gumble's Yard* by John Rowe Townsend

Well, what did you think? Does it work? Is it effective? Why do you think the author wrote that particular beginning and ending?

Activities

1 Have you ever read a book where the ending was a disappointment? This is sometimes called an 'anti-climax'. Make a list of five books you have read where you found the ending disappointing. Compare your list with that of a partner. Does the same book appear on both lists? If so discuss the reasons for your choice.

Now, choose one of the books on your list and rewrite the ending, making it more interesting or satisfying.

2 Choose a book you have read recently and write a different beginning. Perhaps you could make it more exciting, mysterious or intriguing.

3 Not exactly beginnings and endings, but an interesting exercise is a variation of the game, 'Chinese Whispers'. Working in groups of five each person writes a paragraph as the sheet of paper reaches them. When the sheets of paper have been completed there should be five complete short stories. Everyone will have written a beginning, an end and three middle paragraphs.

You might decide to hold a competition to find the best group short story.

3 Story and plot

The power of the imagination

At the beginning of Jan Needle's novel, *My Mate Shofiq*, Bernard Kershaw is making his way to school on a cold, wet morning:

To be quite honest, Bernard hadn't been thinking about trouble that morning. Although it was cold – as cold as charity, whatever that meant – his mind hadn't been thinking about real things much at all. He'd had a problem with his submarine the night before, and he was turning it over and over in his head as he wandered along Middleton Road. Bernard didn't usually bother with his submarine during the day, because it was very much a bed thing, but since his dad had told him that a petrol engine wouldn't work in a sub, because of using up the air, he'd been worrying. He might have to redesign it, quick, or invent a new type of engine. And meanwhile, England might lose the war . . . He was wettish, and chilly up his legs below his anorak, so Bernard decided to run up New Earth Street and round the top of the croft . . . It was there, two hundred yards off the main road, that he saw Whitehead and his lot . . .

He'd stuck his hands in his anorak, and pointed himself towards Cobden Street ('Thirty degrees of port helm on, sir,' because he was a destroyer just at that moment) when he changed his mind again. Bobby Whitehead and his gang weren't looking his way at all, and they were behaving sort of funny. They looked as if they were stalking in their soaking plimsoll-boots. He hunched his shoulders into his neck, he narrowed his eyes and glared along New Earth Street. He became Bernard of the Black Hand.

After a hundred yards or so, it became obvious that Bobby Whitehead's lot were looking for someone definite. They were going dead slow, despite the cold, and they were slinking along like Russian spies. They never looked behind them, which was good, because it made Bernard's task dead easy and dead safe. He nipped from doorway to doorway, dodging past fed-up people slouching off to work, and soon got pretty close. Close enough to see that Bobby and Pat, and at least one of the others, were carrying bricks. They were out to bash someone.

Bernard the Black Hand smiled a sneering smile. Little did they know that an enemy agent had them in his grasp. He patted the Luger under his left armpit. Once let them strike, that's all! Just one false move!

From *My Mate Shofiq* by Jan Needle

We think you will agree that Bernard is certainly a very interesting person with a powerful imagination. Over the distance of only a few hundred yards, he is a submarine designer single-handedly winning the war for England, a naval destroyer, and a Luger-carrying secret agent – and all this on his way to school!

But does any of this make Bernard particularly unusual?

We think not. You see, what Bernard is really doing is making use of the people and places of his surroundings to create his own fantasy world.

In the novel, *Grandad with Snails*, the author, Michael Baldwin, writes about his own childhood, and, as you can see from the following extract, he, too, is used to imagining unusual things happening to him.

The stranger in the light mackintosh lounges negligently against the railings; the darkened car approaches; suddenly miraculously agile, I move: the glass stars in front of the driver's face, the car lurches drunkenly into the kerb. Answering shots bark out from the car, but the occupants are unnerved and shooting wild. Now, masked by an angle in the wall, gripping the notched handle of my Luger, I place my shots with the contempt of long practice. A door opens, a dark shape crumples on to the road. I walk towards the car, and to the alarmed constable who dashes up blowing his whistle I say, 'All right, officer: I'll handle this,' and when he sees the badge on the reverse side of my lapel, he falls back and gapes stupidly. I drag the fallen man into the car. I slide the eyeless driver along the seat and take his place, with scarcely a glance at the shambles in the back, the blood-spattered torn upholstery. As I let the car into gear the constable, suddenly finding his voice, manages to stammer out, 'Good luck, sir!' 'Thanks,' I say. 'I'll need it.' And I roar away to my destiny in the dark. The bus lurched at the crossroads and I came out of my dream. We were running into town, and I was going to get off at the stop by the park.

From *Grandad with Snails* by Michael Baldwin

Now think about yourself for a moment.

Remember the games of Cowboys and Indians or Star Wars in the junior school playground? Ever daydreamed for a few moments in which you have married a prince or princess, scored the winning goal in the last minute of the Cup Final, or won the Miss World beauty competition? Or perhaps you have sat in a cold, miserable classroom and imagined yourself relaxing on a sun-drenched beach, or walked home smug at the thought of beating-up the school bully.

Activity

At this point, we would like you to tell the other members of your group or class about an imaginary adventure in which you have taken the main part. Remember to include all the details of your adventure, and try to tell it in an interesting and exciting manner.

The story

The word 'story' has already occurred several times, and it is important that you understand what it means and are able to recognise it in any work of fiction that you read.

And then . . . and then . . .

In his book, *Aspects of the Novel*, the writer E.M. Forster says that a story is 'a narrative of events arranged in their time sequence' – lunch coming after breakfast, February after January, adolescence after childhood, and so on.

The most important thing to remember about a story is that it relies totally upon time. Try to think in terms of a clock constantly ticking away in the background, counting off the minutes, hours and days as the story unfolds or develops.

How, then, might you tell the story of your life so far today? Perhaps it might read like this:

> I left home at 8 o'clock and then I walked to the bus stop and then I caught a bus at 8.15 and then I arrived in school at 8.35 and then I went to assembly at 8.55 and then I began my first lesson at 9.10 and then . . . and then . . .

It would be possible to continue writing like this to cover all the events for the remainder of your day, using the passage of time to dictate the order of sequence. You could even draw a time-line to show this sequence of events:

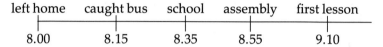

left home	caught bus	school	assembly	first lesson
8.00	8.15	8.35	8.55	9.10

But if, when you arrive home this evening, someone asks you, 'Anything happen today?', you are likely to pick out particular events to describe or retell. You see, there has been something else in your day other than just the passage of time, something which is not measured in minutes and hours.

The value factor

E.M. Forster gave a name to this 'something': he called it 'value', and it is this 'value factor' which enables you to look back over your day and to see it like a graph with a large number of average or ordinary points, and one or two high points. It is the high points that you are most likely to want to talk about when asked the question, 'Anything happen today?'

An example of a graph showing the ordinary and the high points for part of one day is shown below.

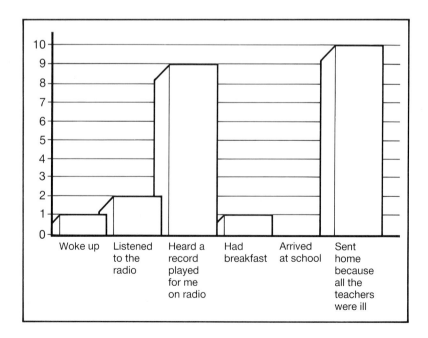

Activity   Think carefully about the sequence of events that made up
your life yesterday.
(a) Draw a time-line to show this sequence of events.
(b) Draw a graph where points 0 to 5 represent average or
    ordinary events and points 6 to 10 represent the day's
    highs.
(c) Write a brief account of your life yesterday, concentrat-
    ing on the high points of the day.

We hope you can see from all of this that daily life is actually
made up of two lives – in Forster's terms, the 'life in time'
and the 'life by values'.
   These terms are important for your study of literature
because:

● What the story does is to tell or narrate the life in time.
● What the novel does is to follow the sequence of the life in
   time, but it includes the life by values as well.

For the moment let us concentrate on what we have called
the 'story'.

What if?
The word 'story' comes from the Latin word *historia* which in
turn comes from a Greek word meaning 'inquiry'.
   Inquiry into what?
   Inquiry into anything and everything.
   The word 'fiction' comes from the Latin *fingere*, meaning to
fashion or form.
   We can say, therefore, that the writer or teller of a fiction
story *inquires* into something and then *fashions* or *forms* that
something into something else.
   Sounds confusing when we put it like that, doesn't it?
   Let's try it another way. Instead of using the word
'inquire', we could use the phrase, 'What if?':

What if I'd missed the bus this morning?
What if I'd lived in the nineteenth century?
What if I were playing football for England this evening?
What if my home burns to the ground today?
What if I am given an elephant for a birthday present?
What if I start shrinking tomorrow?

You've probably already started *forming* or *fashioning*
answers to these questions in your mind.

In other words, you've started to *inquire* into the possibility of something happening under certain circumstances. Using your imagination, you have begun to think out one or more responses or solutions to the question 'What if?' Perhaps without realising it, then, you have begun to construct a fiction story.

Activity

Concentrate for a few moments on the question, 'What if I start shrinking tomorrow?'

Think about the problems and difficulties you would have with clothes or furniture; the kitchen and bathroom would become very awkward places indeed.

Make a list of ten difficulties you would encounter in your home. Compare your list with that of your partner. What similarities and differences are there between your respective lists? Have you left out anything your partner considers important?

You have then *inquired* into the possibilities of starting to shrink and have *fashioned* or *formed* responses to these possibilities.

Once upon a time . . .

What has all of this to do with the study of literature? In this book we are primarily concerned with one particular form of literature: that is, the novel, and whilst there are several different kinds of novel – detective, romantic, mystery, science fiction – they all have one thing in common: the story. The story is what holds a novel together. The story is what we read it for in the first place.

Books and hooks

Books and readers are very much like fishing rods and fish. Because the purpose of every good book is to catch readers, it should come equipped with a hook – that is, with something that grips the reader and holds him wriggling on the end through all the pages.

We know that the novel contains a story. We also know that the story is a narrative of events arranged in their time sequence. As such, the story performs a function similar to that of the skeleton in the human body. Take away the bones and you would collapse into a rather messy and uninteresting blob of jelly on the floor. Take away the story from a novel and you would be left with a shapeless mass of words and there would be nothing to make you wonder, 'What will happen next?'

None of this is in doubt, but is it enough to command the interest of a reader? Is it enough to keep him wriggling on the end of the hook all through all the pages?

From what we have said so far, we hope that you can now confidently answer 'No' to these questions.

In order to qualify and support this answer, we need to return to E.M. Forster's idea of daily life being made up of two elements – the life in time and the life by values – so as to introduce you to another literary term: the plot.

The plot

Look very carefully at the following example which we hope will show you the difference between a story and a plot:

'The husband died and then the wife died' is a story.

'The husband died and then the wife died of grief' is a plot.

The difference between the two sentences is that in the second one a reason is given for the death of the wife.

The time sequence remains intact, but now we have something else to catch our interest – the reason for the wife's death.

Consider the death of the wife: if it is in a story we say, 'And then?'; if it is in a plot we ask, 'Why?'

This, then, represents the main difference between the story and the plot of the novel.

So, the 'hook' that a writer dangles in order to catch and hold his audience consists of more than just a story. It is a hook made up of four different parts and these are:

1 a selection of events arranged in time;
2 events that are interesting in themselves;
3 events that lead naturally to other equally interesting and exciting events;
4 events that have stated reasons and results.

It is the sum total of these parts that we refer to as the plot.

Now look at this example of what we are talking about.

Event	Reason	Result
You run away from home.	You've had a row with your parents.	You are found by the police sleeping rough in a park.

Being found by the police leads naturally on to the next event. The police telephone your home (event) because they want your parents to collect you from the police station (reason). Your parents arrive at the police station (result).

Event	Reason	Result
The police telephone your home.	They want your parents to collect you from the police station.	Your parents arrive at the police station.

Activity

Now continue the plot outline beginning 'You run away from home' by including at least five more events along with their reasons and results. Compare your plot outline with that of your partner. What similarities and differences are there in your responses to this line of inquiry?

Now look at this outline:

> A poor man lives with his wife and baby son in a village. The man finds a precious object. The man, woman and child leave the village. The baby dies. The man and his wife return to the village.

Doesn't sound very interesting, does it? But watch how a good writer can turn the story into a real plot, one in which there are reasons for, and results of, the events.

> Kino, a poor Indian fisherman, lives with his wife and baby son in a village on the outskirts of a town. One morning, the baby is stung by a scorpion. Kino's wife, Juana, is afraid that the baby might die, and they walk to the town to try to get the European doctor to treat their son. The doctor, however, is a greedy, selfish man, and will not treat poor peasants who cannot afford to pay for his services. Kino and Juana have therefore to return to their village angry, ashamed and empty-handed. When Kino next goes diving, he finds a pearl of remarkable size and beauty – 'The Pearl of the World' – and he and Juana are overjoyed at their great fortune. Immediately news of Kino's find spreads throughout the region and everyone begins to consider what Kino's pearl might mean to them. The local priest, who is hoping for a contribution towards

his church, visits Kino. Then the doctor arrives, to fake a temporary sickness in the child so that he can return and supposedly cure it. Kino is suspicious of these visits, and this suspicion is confirmed later that night when someone tries to steal the pearl from his house. The next day he takes his find to the pearl-buyers in the town, expecting to sell it for a large sum of money. But the buyers have agreed between themselves to try and cheat Kino by offering him a low price. Kino becomes angry when he hears their offers and he refuses to sell the pearl, for he sees visions in it of a wonderful future for himself and his family. Because the pearl really is very valuable, further attempts are made to steal it from him.

Juana becomes worried for their safety, and begs her husband to throw the pearl back into the sea. But Kino, obsessed by his visions of a wonderful future, refuses, and he physically attacks his wife when she tries secretly to throw away the pearl. Then he himself is attacked again and this time he kills a man in defending his pearl. Kino and Juana realise that they must leave the village at once since no explanation of theirs about the killing will be accepted by the revengeful men of the town. Kino then discovers that his canoe has been smashed and his house set alight. Concerned now to preserve himself and his family, Kino shelters in the house of his brother, Juan Tomas. The latter goes out among the neighbours to divert their suspicions so that it is widely rumoured that the family has died in the fire or has put out to sea and been drowned. Because of all that has happened, Kino is now even more determined not to give up his pearl, and under cover of darkness the family sets out for the north with the intention of selling the pearl in the city. They make a long and difficult journey into the mountains, with Kino trying hard to hide their trail from their enemies. They are followed by expert trackers who are intent on killing them and stealing the pearl. Realising in desperation that he cannot escape from the trackers, Kino decides to attack and kill them during the night. However, in the ensuing struggle, one of the trackers fires a rifle and shoots Kino's baby. Kino kills the men.

Grief-stricken, Kino and Juana return to their village carrying the body of their child. They walk down to the water's edge and throw the pearl back into the sea where it disappears from view.

The plot of Steinbeck's novel, *The Pearl*, is now much more interesting.

Can you explain why?

Obviously your answer to this question should include comments on the choice of events, and the reasons for, and results of, these events.

Activity   Draw three columns in your exercise book as shown on page 31, and complete the columns using the information given in the plot summary of *The Pearl*.

One of the difficulties you may experience when reading a novel for school is how to keep a brief but accurate record of the book's plot. The above method of using three columns is certainly one idea to consider.

Activity   Select one chapter or section from the novel you are reading at the moment, and represent the events, reasons and results using the method shown above.

Alternatively, you might consider using a box summary to provide a record of the book's plot. Here is a box summary for Anne Holm's novel, *I Am David*, which deals with a boy's long and dangerous journey across Europe following his escape from a concentration camp.

1 David is helped to escape from camp. Expects to be recaptured. Avoids people. Stows away on ship in Salonica. Discovered and helped by sailor. Drifts ashore on lifebelt. Discovers the beauty of things. Realises does not want to die.	2 Washes with soap. Remembers the camp and Johannes. Realises he knows nothing about himself. Makes up a story about a circus. Overhears townspeople discussing him. Afraid of recapture, he sets off northward.
3 David loses his compass. Chooses his 'God'. Helps English holidaymakers. Finds mirror. Given money by American tourists. Hitches to Perugia in lorry.	4 David is attacked by strange boy. Rescues Maria. Enters a house for first time. New clothes. Decides to stay with the family.

5 Finds it difficult to relate to people. Refuses to play soldiers and prisoners. Dislikes Carlo. Overhears parents talking and decides to leave immediately. Maria gives him gold cross.	6 Travels on. Talks to a priest about God. Works on Milan station. Sees newspaper message from Maria's parents. Is afraid of soldiers at a frontier. Meets Sophie who tells him tragic story of woman called Edith.
7 Realises Edith is his mother. Determined to reach Denmark. Spends winter working on farm. Is treated like a prisoner. Befriends a dog. Escapes and crosses into Germany.	8 Writes letter to Carlo. Meets Graf. Runs when thinks he will be recaptured. Dog is killed. Reaches Denmark hidden in a lorry. Finds his mother's house. Is reunited with her.

Activity

Use the box summary method to keep a record of the main events of the plot of a book you are reading.

In this chapter, we have shown you the difference between the terms 'story' and 'plot', and we have given you certain guidelines as to how to deal with the plot structures of your own reading books.

Comprehension
The following comprehension questions are designed to reinforce your understanding of the chapter.

1 Complete this definition: 'A story is a narrative of events . . .'

2 We gave you 'February after January' as one example of the meaning of E.M. Forster's definition of a story. Now write down three further examples of your own; set them out like this:
. . . . . after . . . . .

3 Name one method you could use to show a sequence of events.

4 Forster claims that daily life is actually made up of two lives – what does he call these two lives?

5 How many different kinds of novel can you name?

6 Using your own words, explain how books and readers are very much like fishing rods and fish.

7 Explain in your own words how you would try to make an account of your life history as interesting as possible for a stranger.

8 A plot is made up of four different parts. What are they?

9 Name two things used by a good writer to turn a story into a plot.

10 Name one method you can use to keep a record of a book's plot.

Before we move on to the next chapter, we would like you to consider the following activities. We do not suggest that you attempt every activity, but rather that you select those that are best suited to your own text and purpose.

Activities

1 The writers of comics use both words and pictures when they are telling a story in a comic strip. The words usually appear in what we call 'speech bubbles'. Now draw a comic strip to show the main stages of some part of the action from your own book.

2 Does one of the characters in your book 'disappear' from the action for a period of time before returning at a later stage in the book? If so, write a new chapter for the book in which you describe what you think might have happened to this character in the meantime. Alternatively, extend the plot structure of the novel by adding one completely new chapter, remembering to keep to the existing story line and characters.

3 Design two pages of newspaper reports dealing with one or more of the main events of your plot. One page should be in the style of a sensationalist popular daily paper such as the *Sun* or *Mirror*; the other page should be more in line with the style you would expect to find in *The Times* or the *Guardian*.

4 Imagine that the author of your book decides to write a second novel using some or all of the same main characters. Working in groups of three or four, plan out a suitable plot structure for the new novel: try to decide what you will deal with in each individual chapter, and write brief box summaries using the example given for *I Am David*.

5 Make up a quiz concerned with the people and events from a novel you have read recently. Aim to write at least twenty questions and answers that could be used to test the knowledge of someone else who had read the book.

6 Select one important chapter or section of your book, and draft a play or radio script to show the main events.

7 Select one chapter from your novel and devise a way of displaying the essential storyline of that chapter in a visually interesting and forceful manner using a single large sheet of paper. If there are enough people in your class, it might be possible to deal with a complete book using this method. The completed sheets could then be mounted as a classroom display.

8 Script an edition of TV's 'News at Ten'. Base some of the items on events and incidents from your novel. Other items will be fictional, but should use information and background from the novel.

9 Devise a crossword based on the novel you are reading at the moment. If you have the time you might decide to do a quick crossword and a cryptic crossword.

10 Choose one event from the novel you are reading at the moment and write down the main happenings. Working in small groups dramatise the event by each member of the group assuming the role of one of the characters from the book. It is not essential for members of the group to know the book – in fact, it might be more interesting if they don't.

4 Backgrounds and settings

The setting or background of a novel is never accidental; it must have a purpose. As with real life we are all influenced by our setting, our environment, and there is an obvious link in a novel between the characters and their setting.

There are, in fact, as many different backgrounds and settings in the world of novels as there are in the real world (and in some instances more if we consider science fiction and fantasy). Consider the novels you have read recently. List the different backgrounds and settings that the author uses. Can you think of reasons why authors choose particular settings – or combinations of settings – for their novels? Have you ever read a book that you think would have benefited from a different background or setting?

Here is a checklist of various backgrounds and settings. Can you think of any more?

Backgrounds and settings	
a small town	poverty and squalor
a large city	under the sea
several countries	in the air
inside a building or house	another planet or solar system
a garden	exotic or romantic
someone's imagination	occupational
wealth and luxury	historical

Of course a novel may include more than just one of the above settings; it could be a combination of several.

Activity   Choose three of the above settings and make a list of all the books you've read that use that particular background. You may wish to set your work out as follows:

Historical	Another planet	A garden
Eagle of the North	*Elidor*	*The Secret Garden*

Unusual setting

Consider the following extracts:

A

> The air around the second planet of the Frogstar system was stale and unwholesome. The dank winds that swept continually over its surface swept over salt flats, dried up marshland, tangled and rotting vegetation and the crumbling remains of ruined cities. No life moved across its surface. The ground, like that of many planets in this part of the Galaxy, had long been deserted.
>
> The howl of the wind was desolate enough as it gusted through the old decaying houses of the cities; it was more desolate as it whipped about the bottoms of the tall black towers that swayed uneasily here and there about the surface of this world. At the top of these towers lived colonies of large, scraggy, evil smelling birds, the sole survivors of the civilization that once lived here.

From *The Restaurant at the End of the Universe* by Douglas Adams

B

> Even with eyes protected by green spectacles Dorothy and her friends were at first dazzled by the brilliancy of the wonderful City. The streets were lined with beautiful houses all built of green marble and studded everywhere with sparkling emeralds. They walked over a pavement of the same green marble and where the blocks were joined together were rows of emeralds, set closely, and glittering in the brightness of the sun. The window panes were of green glass; even the sky above the city had a green tint, and the rays of the sun were green . . .
>
> Dorothy's room had a soft, comfortable bed that had sheets of green silk and a green velvet counterpane. There was a tiny fountain in the middle of the room, that shot a spray of green perfume into the air, to fall back into a beautifully carved green marble basin.

From *Journey Through Oz* by L. Frank Baum

C

> Beyond him the road climbed another hill and upon the crest spruce trees bent in the wind and shadows spread like dark water seeping from the mountainside. The ruffled edges of the clouds had turned gold and for a moment it seemed the whole world had become golden, the dried slopes about him reflecting

the coming sunset. He was used to being out of doors at all hours but he had never seen anything like this and he stood, swaying wearily, caught by its splendour. In the distance, off to his right, a herd of deer driven from the higher ridges by the first signs of winter moved slowly across the bronze grass. Except for birds, they were the first signs of life he had seen in days of struggling through this country, and suddenly the enormity of the space around him and the loneliness of its silence became more than he could stand and he found himself running towards the animals, leaving the road and scrambling over sun-scorched pasture land in a fury of haste.

From *The Loner* by Ester Wier

Activities

1 Read through the extracts again and make a list of all the words that illustrate the way in which the author informs us of the three different settings. You may wish to set your work out as follows:

Extract A	Extract B	Extract C
stale	dazzled	golden
unwholesome	brilliancy	splendour
dank	wonderful	bronze grass
dried up	beautiful	silence
tangled	green marble	sun-scorched

Discuss your list with a partner. Have you both extracted the same words?

2 Take a passage from a book you are reading at the moment that deals with place or setting. Now, extract all the words and phrases that describe either the physical nature of the place or the atmosphere created, or both.

3 Working with a partner, make a list of words that could be used to describe a particular setting or background. Write a short description using all the words in the list and then do the same for the list of words written by your partner.

When you have finished compare your descriptions with those of your partner. Are there any similarities or differences?

Normal setting, unusual or misplaced characters

Ahead of her stretched a long, well lit hallway. Its ceiling and walls were a smoothly curved arch, its floor hard and flat, with a soft layer of carpet down the middle. The light came from the walls, where every foot or so on both sides a tiny light bulb had been recessed and the hole in which it stood, like a small window, had been covered with a square of coloured glass – blue green or yellow. The effect was that of stained glass windows in sunlight.

The room they entered was big, square, well lit, and had a faint musty smell. 'It's reasonably comfortable, and if you like to read . . .' he gestured at the walls. They were lined with shelves from floor to ceiling, and on the shelves stood – Mrs Frisby dredged in her memory. 'Books,' she said. 'They're books. A library.'

Activity

Working with a partner, discuss the sort of book that you think the extract above comes from. What do you think the story is about? What sort of person do you think Mrs Frisby is?

Of course, you may have recognised that the extract is taken from *Mrs Frisby and the Rats of NIMH* by Robert C. O'Brien and that Mrs Frisby is a field mouse, but perhaps you didn't. Mrs Frisby is on a visit to the rats to ask for their help. If you didn't already know the story we don't think you would have guessed you were reading about mice and rats. The setting is only unusual insomuch as the characters involved are animals. Had the characters been human, the setting would have been perfectly normal, even mundane.

Can you think of any other examples where it is the characters that make the setting unusual?

Describing landscape

The Yorkshire moors are strange and lovely places. Sometimes they are soft and gentle. The birds sing and the breezes are kind on your face. But sometimes they are different. They are harsh and cruel, strong and unwelcoming. The mist falls swiftly and quite silently. Almost at once, with little or no warning, you are lost in a thick white cloud and your sense of direction vanishes unless you know your way about. Lost in the mist, it is like the end of the world. There is no one there.

From *Wild Boy* by Joan Tate

The great bog which lies at the heart of Dartmoor is a silent place. Few birds fly there and the streams flow quietly between barks of black peat, or lose themselves in morasses of moss and rushes. For many miles you can walk, and hear only the sound of the wind in the heather, and the sullen splash of your own feet in the black water. On a fine, sunny day, this silence is pleasant, a release from the noise of the world; under grey skies, it is grim and threatening.

From *The Wish Hounds* by Kathleen Hunt

Activities

1 Would you want to visit one of the above places? Can you say why?

2 Working with a partner, discuss the differences and similarities between the three passages.

3 Give a verbal description to your partner of a place you both know well. Your partner must guess what or where the place is. How evocative of the place was the description? Did it include all the details concerning the place?

Urban setting

If you live in an inner-city area, you may recognise this type of setting from the beginning of *Gumble's Yard*:

It was a fine spring day, not warm but with a sort of hazy sunshine, and I was walking through the Jungle with my sister Sandra and my friend Dick. The Jungle isn't a real jungle, it's a district off the Wigan Road in the city of Cobchester. We call it the Jungle because all the streets are named after tropical flowers – like Orchid Grove, where we live. That may sound gay and colourful, but there's nothing colourful about the Jungle. It's a dirty old place, and one of these days the Corporation are going to pull it all down – if it doesn't fall down of its own accord first.

From *Gumble's Yard* by John Rowe Townsend

Activities

1 From the brief description you have been given, write a paragraph about the housing conditions to be found in Orchid Grove.

2 Imagine that some friends are coming to stay with you and you are unable to meet them at the station. You must, therefore, write some instructions for them to follow. They must be clear and accurate, but you must give the impression that where you live is more atmospheric and frightening than Count Dracula's castle.

3 Write two descriptions of the area in which you live. Make one description purely factual, whilst the other should be imaginatively written to create an exciting atmosphere.

Setting and time

Occasionally we are left to work out for ourselves not only the background or setting of the novel but also the time in which it is set. It is important to remember that 'time' in a novel can refer to the time of day, year or period in history. Modern novelists don't usually go in for long passages describing the setting or time of their books. The two main ways of giving the reader information about the time and setting of a novel are:

1 characters talking about the time and setting;

2 keeping the time and setting in the reader's mind by a variety of small, consistent and relevant details.

The country is so flat round there they didn't have to dig embankments for the trains. They just laid the tracks on the ground, and it runs like that for miles . . .

The snow was about a foot deep, but the wind had blown it in drifts, and it was up to your armpits in the drifts. We went in a couple of times, and then steered a wide track round and some time during this Soldier started dropping behind. I heard him yelling and looked round and he was straggling a long way back, so I waited for him. It was pretty ghastly, waiting. I could feel my feet in the snow, icy wet and aching in my plimsolls . . . That must have been some time after one. There were only two hours of daylight left then . . .

There was a wood of conifers at the other side of the road gabled with snow. There were telegraph poles, the wires also heaped with snow. It was a nice snow scene, if you like snow scenes.

From *Run For Your Life* by David Line

In this extract David Line has given you information about the countryside, the weather, the time of year, the time of day and the mood of the character. Make a list of all the words and phrases that give you this information.

Activities

1 Look at the following list and decide what sort of information you are being given about the time or setting, or both. Discuss you answers with a partner.

(a) she looked down in disgust at the sensible brown leather school shoes

(b) his sneakers burned up the tarmac as he raced along the road

(c) taking care not to stain her satin slippers, she carefully avoided the puddles on the stone stairway

(d) he pressed his silicon booted foot hard upon the warp machine's accelerator

(e) he hardly noticed the sun beating down upon his head as he marched along because his new leather boots, with their steel toecaps, cut into his feet

(f) she grunted with satisfaction as she gazed at her newly acquired bearskin boots

(g) the jewels on his high-heeled shoes glittered in the candlelight as he asked Lady Venetia to dance

(h) his hessian rope sandals met with approval from the other members of the commune

2 Now consider the book you are reading at the moment and decide its setting and time. It may, of course, have more than one setting or time, so be prepared. Make a list of the major settings and times. You do not have to be very specific unless you are actually given a date. Then write down one or more examples from the text to support your statements. You may wish to set your work out as shown below.

Title of book:		Author:	
Setting	Supporting details	Time of day/year	Supporting details
Seaside	The warm wet sand. Bright clouds hung over the sea	Victorian	her crinoline was rather cumbersome

Historical setting

The half loft in the crown of the roof was full of warm, crowding shadows through which the bar of fading sunlight from the gap in the roof fell like a golden sword. There was a warm smell of mist and dust, and the sharper, aromatic tang of the dried herbs hanging in bundles from the rafters, and the animal smell of skin rugs laid aside there until the winter. Spare farm tools were stacked deep under the eaves, and the raw, grey-brown bundles of wool from the last clip, and the wicker kists in which the household kept their clothes and gear. Harness hung among the herbs, and a smoked bear ham; and there, too, were the two-handled crocks full of honey that kept the household in sweetness from one bee harvest to the next. At the open side, almost in the smoke of the hearth fire that wreathed past on its way to the smoke hole, hung two shields: Drustic's shield that had been their father's, and the great bull's hide buckler with the bronze bosses that was the Grandfather's and would be Drem's one day . . .

. . . his mother was working at her loom: a big upright loom, the warp threads held taut by a row of triangular clay weights at the bottom.

From *Warrior Scarlet* by Rosemary Sutcliff

Activities Using the above passage, answer the following questions. Use your own words whenever you can.

1 When do you think the novel is set? What evidence is there to support your answer?

2 What time of day is it? What time of year is it? Write down a word or phrase to support your answer.

3 Describe the inside of the dwelling. How does it differ from your home?

4 Make a list of all the words and phrases in the extract that describe weapons or tools.

5 What items were used instead of blankets?

6 Find out the meaning of the following:
kists   bull's hide buckler   bronze bosses
warp threads

Reactions to settings

The author of a novel will make the characters react in various ways to the setting. Look again at the extract from *Run For Your Life* on page 44. Write down how the character feels about his setting. Compare your notes with those of a partner. Are there any similarities or differences?

Now do the same for this longer extract from *A Kestrel for a Knave:*

It was still dark outside when he got up and went downstairs. The living-room curtains were drawn, and when he switched the light on it was gloomy and cold without the help of the fire. He placed the clock on the mantelpiece, then picked up his mother's sweater from the settee and pulled it on over his shirt.

The alarm rang as he was emptying the ashes in the dustbin. Dust clouded up into his face as he dropped the lid back on and ran inside, but the noise stopped before he could reach it. He knelt down in front of the empty grate and scrunched sheets of newspaper into loose balls, arranging them in the grate like a bouquet of hydrangea flowers. Then he picked up the hatchet, stood a nog of wood on the hearth and struck it down the centre. The blade bit and held. He lifted the hatchet with the nog attached and smashed it down, splitting the nog in half and chipping the tile with the blade. He split the halves into quarters, down through eighths to sixteenths, then arranged these sticks over the paper like the struts of a wigwam. He completed the construction with lumps of coal, building them into a loose shell, so that sticks and paper showed through the chinks. The paper caught with the first match, and the flames spread quickly underneath, making the chinks smoke and the sticks crack. He waited for the first burst of flames up the back of the construction, then stood up and walked into the kitchen, and opened the pantry door. There were a packet of dried peas and a half bottle of vinegar on the shelves. The bread bin was empty. Just inside the doorway, the disc of the electricity meter circled slowly in its glass case. The red arrow appeared, and disappeared. Billy closed the door and opened the outside door. On the step stood two empty milk bottles. He thumped the jamb with the inside of his fist.

'It's t'same every morning. I'm going to start hiding some at nights.'

He started to turn inside, then stopped, and looked out again. The garage door was open. He ran across the concrete strip and used the light from the kitchen to look inside.

'Well, of all the rotten tricks!'

He kicked a can of oil the length of the garage and ran back into the house. The coal had caught fire, and the yellow flames were now emitting a slight warmth. Billy pulled his pumps on without unfastening the laces and grabbed his windcheater. The zip was broken and the material draped out behind him as he vaulted the front wall and raced up the avenue.

From *A Kestrel for a Knave* by Barry Hines

Consider the novel you are reading at the moment. Choose one of the main characters and make a list of some of the situations he or she finds himself or herself in. Alongside, write down what the character actually does in each situation, and, if appropriate, his or her feelings about the situation.

Mood indicators

There is another way in which authors sometimes use their settings or backgrounds, and that is to reflect the mood or feelings of the characters involved.

Here is a typical example:

Rocky didn't have to think twice . . . He made his way straight to the Golden Salamander, a misnamed snack bar of anything but a golden appearance off Upper Parliament Street. He went through the streets confidently, his hands thrust into his pockets. He whistled nonchalantly, and strode into the lighted cafe, straight up to the counter above which, unfortunately, his head only just showed.

Venturini, the owner, was a balding Italian. He looked down at Rocky.

'Yes?'

'A plate of chips, some bread 'n' butter, an' a cup of tea.'

Venturini raised his eyebrows. Rocky shrugged and smacked the two shilling piece down on the counter. Then he swaggered to one of the tubular, plastic-topped tables beside the window. The table tops were red, the place was plastered with advertisements, lit with cold neon. Rocky's feet barely touched the floor when he sat down. But he was happy there. He liked the big red plastic bottle that you squeezed tomato sauce out of, and the big salt shakers. He liked to feel he was independent and important – and more than anything he liked the food. It was slid before you on a white bakelite plate – a pile of pale yellow chips, two rounds of bread and butter, a big cup of strong tea. Rocky sprinkled the chips liberally with salt, drowned them in a flowing tide of tomato sauce, and tucked in.

From *A Pair of Jesus-Boots* by Sylvia Sherry

Activity

The scene is a dentist's waiting room and surgery. There are two patients: one is for check-up only, one is for two fillings and an extraction. Fill in a chart like the one shown below, giving what you consider would be their varying descriptions of the same place.

Patient One	Check-up only	Patient Two	Two fillings; extraction
Description of waiting room:		Description of waiting room:	
Description of surgery:		Description of surgery:	

In the following extracts from the same book, the setting and description of the weather reflect the moods of the characters.

A

> Again he put his trembling hands to his head, and gave a wild ringing scream, the cry of desolation. For a few moments after, he stood motionless; but the cry had relieved him from the first maddening pressure of the truth . . .
>
> And now that all the false hopes had vanished, and the first shock of certainty was past, the idea of a thief began to present itself . . . he started from his loom to the door. As he opened it the rain beat in upon him, for it was falling more and more heavily. There were no footsteps to be tracked on such a night – footsteps?

B

> There was one time of the year which was held in Raveloe to be especially suitable for a wedding. It was when the great lilacs and laburnums in the old-fashioned gardens showed their golden and purple wealth above the lichen tinted walls, and when there were calves still young enough to want bucketfuls of fragrant milk . . . It was a time when a light bridal dress could be worn with comfort and seen to advantage.
>
> Happily the sunshine fell more warmly than usual on the lilac tufts the morning that Eppie was married, for her dress was a very light one . . . Seen at a distance as she walked across the churchyard and down the village she seemed to be attired in pure white, and her hair looked like the dash of gold on a lily.

From *Silas Marner* by George Eliot

Activity

(a) What sort of atmosphere is evoked by the first extract?
(b) What sort of atmosphere is evoked by the second extract?
(c) How does the author create the differing atmospheres?
(d) In what ways do the extracts reflect the mood of each character?
(e) Working with a partner, try and find as many examples as you can where their background/setting or weather, or both, reflect the mood or feelings of the characters. You may use the book you are reading at the moment and any other novel you have read in the past.

Extended activities

1 If you had to choose one place or setting from a book you have read in which to spend the rest of your life, where would you choose and why?

2 Working with a partner, select a book that you both know well and devise a way of displaying the background or setting of the book in a visually interesting and forceful manner using a single large sheet of paper.

3 Many authors have the ability to create a very effective atmosphere in their novels. Have you ever been anywhere that had a distinctly unpleasant atmosphere? Write a description of such a place, remembering to include the colours, sounds and smells that contributed towards the atmosphere.

4 Using the background details from a novel you have read, draw a map or sketch of one of the places in the book.

5 The past and future are very popular as settings for novels. If you could move backwards or forwards in time which way would you go? Choose a particular year in the past or future and imagine you are interviewing a person for today's papers. What is their life like? What hobbies or interests do they have? What sort of food do they eat? Do they have schools? Add any other questions that you think are relevant.

6 Imagine that you have been invited by your school to leave a time capsule buried in the grounds. Make a list of all the things you would include and give reasons for your choice. You must also include five books that you feel would be of interest to people in the future.

7 Choose a book you have read recently. Imagine that you become a character in the novel and find yourself in one of the settings. Describe this setting in detail.

8 Working with a partner, prepare a short talk that describes the view from your classroom window: (a) 200 years ago, and (b) 200 years in the future.

9 Have you ever dreamt of a place that you feel you would know well if you ever went there? Describe such a place in detail.

10 Working in small groups devise a 'Twenty Questions' game based on settings, backgrounds or places. The team can ask any questions to try and discover what the place or setting is. The person answering the questions can only answer yes or no.

5 Characters

Where do they come from?

The characters in a good novel are interesting, intriguing, consistent, convincing, complex and realistic. If the author has created a particularly vivid or individualistic character, then we, as readers, will find that character interesting regardless of whether or not we sympathise with him or her.

Activities

Look carefully at the following activities. They are fairly short and can be tackled orally, or as a written exercise.

1 Write down the names of all the characters from the novel you are reading at the moment. Now, next to each name write down just one fact about that character.

2 Write down the name of the character you have found the most interesting from a book you have read. Then write down five facts about that character.

3 Working in small groups, each member of the group should read out the name of their character, the book the character appears in and the five facts. The other members of the group are then allowed to ask questions about that character, so be prepared to justify your choice and to give details.

4 Ask your teacher or a member of your family to tell you about their favourite characters. Can they explain why they chose them?

5 What sort of characters do you prefer? Characters of your own age? Sensible, intelligent characters? Characters that always seem to be in trouble? Discuss your choices with a partner.

Creating characters

Look at the sketch. Believe it or not but this is how some people think authors create characters. Finding arms and legs and other bits and fitting them together, and in some ways they are correct. It is rather like the idea of Frankenstein creating his monster, although, hopefully, not many of the characters you meet in this chapter will be quite so destructive!

When you write an essay you create the characters involved. You have made them from the various materials you have in your possession, your imagination, your knowledge of the people around you, your ideas concerning how people will act in certain situations, and various other factors.

Authors use the same process when they are creating characters for their novels.

Activity

In small groups, discuss what it is about characters that make them seem believable. Try to isolate the factors that make the characters from a book seem like real people.

Types of characters

Of course, characters are common to all novels, but there is an infinite variety of characters. Rather as in the real world where, as the saying goes, 'It takes all sorts,' you will find lots of different types of characters in most novels. The author will actually supply you with the details you need to establish what type of character they are.

Later on in this chapter we will discuss how the author actually reveals his characters to the reader, but for now let us consider 'types' of characters.

When you were young, you were probably told many fairy tales. Such tales tend to have very simple characters in them. In fact, you could actually divide them into just two types:

the goodies
the baddies.

As we get older and read more complex stories, the characters can no longer be easily divided into 'good' or 'bad' categories.

We have compiled below a short, but by no means complete, list of character types. Add to the list whenever you come across another 'type' of character.

Type	Function
Ornaments	for decoration and enjoyment, might be comic characters.
Secretaries	generally to pass on information.
Ears	to listen to the other characters – perhaps to give the main character a reason for telling their story.
Critics	to give the author a means by which to state his views about people or situations.

Rounded or flat?

Discuss with a partner the type of characters that appear in the novel you are reading at the moment. Do any of them fit into the above categories? If so, these are what are known as 'flat' characters. Do any of the characters have more than one function? Are there any characters that appear to be different types at different times?

We hope that the answer to the last two questions was 'yes', because the next section depends entirely upon a 'yes' answer. If a character is a different type at different times he or she is not a 'flat' character. Such characters have more than one function or idea. They are 'rounded' and have many and varied characteristics. They are a mixture of different elements. Just like you!

We are all a mixture of attributes both good and bad, pleasant and unpleasant. These 'rounded' characters are usually the main characters in a book.

Activity   Working with a partner, make a list of five of your good points and five of your bad points. Do the same for your partner. When you have both finished, discuss your lists. Do you agree on any points? Are there any differences?

Below are three descriptions of different characters. Read them carefully.

A

Mr Hazel was a pie and sausage manufacturer with an unbelievably arrogant manner. He was rich beyond words, and his property stretched for miles along either side of the valley. He was a self-made man, with no charm at all and precious few virtues. He loathed all persons of humble station, having once been one of them himself, and he strove desperately to mingle with what he believed were the right kind of folk. He hunted with the hounds and gave shooting parties and wore fancy waistcoats, and every weekday he drove an enormous black Rolls-Royce past the filling station on his way to and from the factory.

From *Danny The Champion of the World* by Roald Dahl

B

I saw him at the end of the street, a white scarf, pallid face under a dim hat, a spare body moving to me in sailor's jacket and heavy trousers, one hand hanging free, one holding a square case. I bumped into his legs and looked down. The slit shoes were there as always. His hand fell on my shoulder and his voice said, 'Hello, Cockie.'

'Hello, Boss,' I said. I looked up at the eyes and saw the lips twist under the moustache. The face knotted for a moment on a breath. The smile came back, and we stood with the rain streaming off us. He lifted me onto his shoulder and I was his pilot through the weather till we got back home.

Nan came out, and Mum and Dad, from the oven roast of the room. 'Look at that boy: he's soaked to the skin.'

'I called him down to me,' said the Boss with a quick lie. He took off his cap, his scarf, and his coat; and there he was in the sort of grey-white pepper and salt pullover he always wore, and the pullover was tucked into trousers that came almost under his armpits, jacked up on wide braces of the old fashioned 'Quick release' sort ('Have to use the lavatory on board ship without stopping, boy'). Round his waist, a good nine inches under his trouser tops, was a broad black belt.

'Why do I still wear a belt and braces together? 'Cos I'm a pessimist, Cockie. A working man's got to be . . .'

From *Grandad With Snails* by Michael Baldwin

C

> He paused to crack his knuckle joints and inspect his Dad.
> The great writer was still in his scruffy old dressing gown and
> smelt of warm bed. The bald top of his head worn thin by the
> great brains, gleamed dully, and his beard was full of fluff. He
> was staring at the cornflake packet as if it was full of bad news.
> He was not in good shape. Perhaps he was unconscious. It
> was often hard to tell . . .
>
> Conrad went into his Dad's room. Conrad's Dad was doing
> his pressups. Conrad watched him. Conrad's Dad could do
> more pressups than Conrad, but he had an unfair advantage,
> Conrad thought. His belly was so fat that it was still on the floor
> supporting him even when his arms were at full stretch. Despite
> this he groaned a lot and went a sometimes frightening colour
> in the face.

From *Conrad's War* by Andrew Davies

The above extracts are examples of three very different types of characters. We now want you to think about each of the characters in turn. What information does the author give you? What conclusions can you draw about each of the characters?

Activity

Look at the example below, which shows how information concerning the character has been extracted from the first passage and then do the same for the other three extracts.

Extract: A   *Character's name:* Mr Hazel

Information: pie and sausage manufacturer
arrogant, self-made
little charm, few virtues
came from a humble background
mingles with the 'right kind of folk'
hunts, gives shooting parties
wears long waistcoats
drives black Rolls-Royce

Opinion of the character:
Mr Hazel is not a very pleasant person at all. He is big-headed and rather snobbish. He has got an enormous amount of money, but this does not make him a sympathetic character. It appears, in fact, that Mr Hazel's money allows him to be horrid to people.

> He has very little consideration for wild life and is prepared to kill animals to improve his social position. He wears flashy clothes and drives a large, expensive car.

We are sure that you will agree that Roald Dahl has chosen his words carefully to make sure that we do not like Mr Hazel.

Now remember to set out your work the same as in the example. When you have finished your extracts, discuss what you have written with a partner. Have you both extracted the same information? Have you both formed the same opinion of the characters?

Characters revealed

Earlier in this chapter we said that we would examine how the author reveals his characters to us, the readers.

Here is a list of the most commonly used means.

Characters are revealed by:
- what they say about themselves
- what other characters say about them
- what the narrator or author says about them
- the reactions of other characters
- the reaction of the characters to certain situations
- the reaction of the characters to their environment
- their physical features and build
- their manner of dress
- their accent or social position
- their attitude to life
- their education
- their habits and mood

Are there any other methods that you can think of, based on your own reading?

Now, consider the following passages:

A

> It's never the wrong time to call on Toad. Early or late he's always the same fellow. Always good tempered, always glad to see you, always sorry when you go. He is indeed the best of animals. So simple, so good natured, and so affectionate. Perhaps he's not very clever – we can't all be geniuses.

B

> ...and his pride and conceit began to swell within him. 'Ho, ho!' he said to himself as he marched along with his chin in the air, 'what a clever Toad I am! There is surely no animal equal to me for cleverness in the whole world!... Ho, ho! I am The Toad, the handsome, the popular, the successful Toad!'

From *The Wind in the Willows* by Kenneth Grahame

The first extract is a description of Toad by one of his friends. The second is a description of Toad by Toad himself. Here Kenneth Grahame has given the reader two very different images of Toad. Throughout the book the author reveals the character of Toad through many devices.

Activity

Now, choose one of the main characters from the novel you are reading at the moment. Look at your checklist and decide which of the various methods listed are used by your author. It might be a good idea to set your work out as shown below.

Method	Example from (insert the title of your book)
(a) What the character states about himself (Other methods) ↓	(Examples) ↓

Sometimes an author reveals his character through another character's analysis of a set of clues. To see what we mean, read the following extract:

> '...Observation with me is second nature. You appeared to be surprised when I told you, on our first meeting, that you had come from Afghanistan.'
> 'You were told, no doubt.'
> 'Nothing of the sort. I *knew* you came from Afghanistan. From long habit the train of thoughts ran so swiftly through my mind that I arrived at the conclusion without being conscious of intermediate steps. There were such steps however. The train

of reasoning ran, "Here is a gentleman of a medical type, but with the air of a military man. Clearly an army doctor, then. He has just come from the tropics, for his face is dark, and that is not the natural tint of his skin, for his wrists are fair. He has undergone hardship and sickness, as his haggard face says clearly. His left arm has been injured. He holds it in a stiff and unnatural manner. Where in the tropics could an English army doctor have seen much hardship and got his arm wounded? Clearly in Afghanistan." The whole train of thought did not occupy a second. I then remarked that you came from Afghanistan, and you were astonished.'

From *A Study in Scarlet* by Sir Arthur Conan Doyle

Activity

Working in small groups, answer the following questions:

1 How did Sherlock Holmes work out that Dr Watson had come from Afghanistan?

2 What clues do you think Sherlock Holmes was able to pick up from Dr Watson's appearance that made it obvious that he was a medical man?

3 What do you think is meant by the phrase 'the air of a military man'?

4 Look carefully at another member of your form. Now, imagine that he or she disappears and you have to write a detailed description of him or her to give to the police.

5 Discuss the accuracy of each description with members of another group.

6 To test the observation skills of each member of the group, take it in turns to describe a teacher you all know well. Do you all agree with the descriptions?

Character reaction and interaction

Let us now look at another major aspect of a good novel: the interaction of the characters. Look again at Extract B on page 54.

'I called him down to me,' said the Boss with a quick lie.

Here we have an example of the actions of one character affecting the actions of another. The Boss thought Nan would be annoyed with the boy so he lied to her. Her action affected the Boss's action.

If we think back to the fairy tales we knew as children, it was the interaction of the good and evil characters that made the story interesting. The contrast between the behaviour of each character is what makes them come alive and enables the reader to believe in them. The characters react to each other and develop throughout a novel, and it is this action and reaction that usually makes up the majority of a good book.

Activity

Look carefully at the extract below and then examine the interaction diagram. Take note of how the arrows represent not only the flow of action and reaction, but also the time sequence.

Herbert said, 'What is it, Pincher?' and turned; he looked at Tom and never saw him.

Edgar had turned quickly, at the same time: he looked more searchingly, through Tom, while the dog at their feet continued his growling. It was very rude of them, Tom felt, and very stupid too. Suddenly he lost patience with the lot of them. He felt the impulse to be rude back, and gave way to it; after all, no one could see him: he stuck out his tongue at them. In retort, the girl Hatty darted out her tongue at Tom. For a moment, Tom was so astounded that he almost believed he had imagined it; but he knew he had not. The girl had stuck her tongue out at him.

She could see him.

'What did you stick out your tongue for, Hatty?' asked Edgar, who must be able to see things even out of the corners of his eyes.

'My tongue was hot in my mouth,' said Hatty, with a resourcefulness that took Tom by surprise. 'It wanted to be cool – it wanted fresh air.'

'Don't give pert, lying answers!'

'Let her be, Edgar,' said James.

They lost interest in the dog's curious behaviour, and in Hatty's. They began to move back to the house. The dog skulked along nervously beside them, keeping them between himself and Tom, and still muttering to himself deep in his throat; the girl walked slightly ahead of them all.

Tom followed, seething with excitement, waiting his chance.

From *Tom's Midnight Garden* by Philippa Pearce

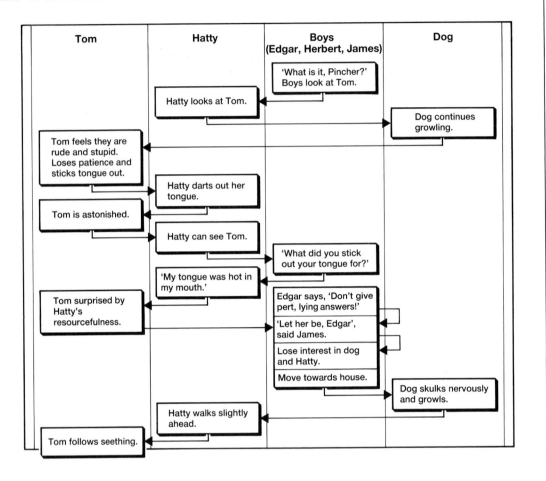

Interaction of the characters

Now choose a passage from the novel you are reading at the moment and represent the actions and reactions between the characters as shown in the example.

Character studies

It may seem strange to you, but we have left what could possibly be described as the most important aspect of the chapter until the end. That is the actual writing of a character study. A well-written character study should contain details of physical appearance, dress, attitude, personality, reaction to the environment and the interaction of the character with other characters in the novel. Obviously every character study is going to contain very different information, but the basic plan remains the same.

Activity Read the following description carefully:

> She was a slender creature, small for her age, but rosy cheeked, with a mass of tumbled black locks falling to her shoulders, and two brilliant blue eyes, equally ready to dance with laughter or flash with indignation. Her square chin also gave promise of a powerful and obstinate temper, not always perfectly controlled. But her mouth was sweet and she could be very thoughtful on occasions.

From *The Wolves of Willoughby Chase* by Joan Aiken

Copy the chart below. In each of the seven columns, fill in suitable words from the passage. Some have already been completed for you.

Build	Features	Hair	Eyes	Voice	Habits	Personality
slender small			brilliant blue that flash			thoughtful

Now choose three people you know particularly well and complete a chart for each of them. When you have finished your charts, choose one and write a character study. Remember to include all the details contained in your chart and examples of incidents involving the character to illustrate your character study.

Hopefully you are now in possession of all the skills you need to write detailed character studies about any of the characters in your book.

Extended activities

1 Take one of the main characters from the novel you are reading at the moment and 'adopt' him or her. Now write the name of the character across a double-page spread. As you read through your book, make a note of all the occasions when your character appears, is mentioned, is thought about or talked about – by himself or

by others. When you have finished reading the novel, use the information contained in your list of comments and quotations to write a detailed character study.

2 Using a chart, plot the interaction between all the main characters in the book you are reading at the moment. You will only be able to record the major incidents, remember. If you have forgotten how to do this, turn back to page 60 to refresh your memory.

3 Script the interview between yourself and the character you would most like to meet from any book you have read.

4 Script the encounter between two of your favourite characters from literature. It may be interesting to dramatise the script when it is written.

5 Set up a quiz, in which the members of each team have to answer questions about characters from various books.

6 Choose a character from a historical novel and imagine you have to show him or her the sights of your town or city. Plan your day to include as many interesting events as possible. Then write an account of the day from the character's point of view.

7 Choose a really nasty character from a novel you have read recently. Make a list of all the reasons why you disliked him or her and say in what way they influenced the other characters in the book.

8 Sometimes when we watch a film of a book we have read the characters seem different to how we imagined them. Why do you think this is so? Discuss your answers with a partner.

9 Working with a partner choose a character from a book you have both read. Each of you write a description of the character and then choose the actor or actress you would want to play the part. Discuss your description and choice with your partner. Are your descriptions similar? Have you both chosen the same actor or actress?

10 Working in small groups, each choose a character from a book you have all read. Now, imagine that each of these characters is on trial for his or her place in the novel. Each member of the group has to justify why they should retain their place. The character with the most convincing argument wins.

6 *Themes in life and literature*

When Conrad came down for breakfast and explained his idea of making a sort of tank, he became annoyed because, as usual, his Dad didn't pay any attention.

That night, Mr Pike was watching television in the living room when—

There was an immensely satisfying musical shattering sound, and the whole French window caved in and fell on the carpet. The Centurian nosed deafeningly on, crushing and splintering glass, wood and bricks, and Conrad halted it when its nose touched the opposite wall. It filled the living room almost completely . . .

'What about THAT then DAD??' shouted Conrad.

'Fantastic,' said his Dad. 'I have to admit it.'

. . . There was no doubt about it. Conrad had really impressed his Dad at last.

From *Conrad's War* by Andrew Davies

Thankfully, we don't always have to go to such extremes to impress other people with our ideas.

But how exactly *do* we get our ideas across?

Activity   Think for a few minutes about any ideas you have had recently. Jot them down, and then explain to your partner how you set about getting other people interested in them. What techniques did you use? Were you successful?

Communicating ideas

When a writer has an idea he wants to share with other people, he will communicate it using the form of a novel, play or poem.

John Steinbeck, the author of *The Red Pony* said that the idea for the book came from personal experience:

> 'It was written,' said Steinbeck, 'at a time when there was desolation in my family. The first death had occurred. And the family, which every child believes to be immortal, was shattered. Perhaps this is the first adulthood of any man or woman. The first tortured question "Why?" and then acceptance, and then the child becomes a man. *The Red Pony* was an attempt . . . to set down this loss and acceptance and growth.'

Activity   Think back to those ideas you jotted down for the previous activity.

(a) Can you remember what inspired them?
(b) Were any of them based on experiences you had had earlier?
(c) If not, what *were* they based on?

Steinbeck says that 'the first death had occurred' in his family. He goes on to describe the family as being 'shattered'. Clearly, a child faced with this experience has a number of problems to overcome, but then, life is like that, isn't it?

Or is it? How do we know?

Have you even given the matter much thought before today?

To be honest, there was a time when we would have had difficulty with those questions. But now we know more about the situation because we have read *The Red Pony*. This tells the story of Jody, a young farmboy, his longing for a horse of his own and his first encounters with the harsh realities of life.

Having read the story of Jody, we think we are more *aware* of the problems and difficulties facing a young person in his situation.

The important thing to realise, of course, is that this increased general awareness has come from reading a story about one particular individual.

Story and theme

We can express this better by using the words 'story' and 'theme'. Look at this example:

The Dangerous Ones
by Vernon Scannell

Story
Robert is fifteen and restless. He is fascinated and excited by Dick Steele and his sister Cindy and the glamorous life they seem to offer. He is flattered by their 'friendship' and, falling under their dangerous influence, is brought to the brink of serious crime.

Theme
Vernon Scannell has a natural understanding of the problems that confront the young in our materialist society. He writes with pace and feeling – a feeling for Robert as he discovers what we all come to learn, that 'within every one of us there exists a judge, jailer and executioner'.

These two paragraphs come from a publisher's blurb, though they didn't appear under separate headings because publishers assume that we can differentiate between 'story' and 'theme'.

You are probably aware that there are as many different themes in literature as there are in life. Here are some examples:

Man's inhumanity to man.
Ambition and greed.
The generation gap.

Activities

1 How many other examples can you think of based on your recent reading? Make a list and compare it with that of your partner. What similarities and differences are there in your lists? Do these tell you anything about your reading preferences?

2 Organise a competition in your group to find the largest number of different literary themes over a period of, say, a week. You need not have read the books concerned, but your lists should contain the titles and authors.

3 Do some themes appear more often than others? Devise a chart to show the popularity of different themes.

4 Select one theme, such as, say, the problem of racialism in modern society, and make a list of all those novels you can find dealing with that theme.

Many books contain more than one theme or idea. Look at the example below of Jack Schaefer's first Western, *Shane*.

The story is quite straightforward: the brave, dashing hero comes from no one knows where, takes up the cause of the weak and oppressed against the rich powerful 'villain'. He fights a battle with the 'villain', and kills him, thereby restoring peace and harmony. Then he rides off and is never seen again.

The basic theme is an old one: the forces of good struggle with and overcome the forces of evil. But there are at least two other themes in the novel:

1 The theme of maturing: the young boy in the novel is made aware of complex emotions that without Shane's visit he would not have known until much later.

2 The theme of choice and decision: Shane's choice of direction at a fork in the road brings him to the Starrett ranch, and sets in motion a series of events which changes the course of many lives as the characters 'decide' on their responses to his arrival. As a result understandings and insights are discovered.

Activities

1 Look again at your novel. Does it have any other themes apart from the main one?

2 Here are some more blurbs about novels. Decide with your partner which sentences are concerned with the

'story' and which deal with the 'theme' or 'themes'. In each case, write down the theme(s) of the book, using your own words as far as possible.

A

> When Sumitra's family is kicked out of Uganda because they are Asians not Africans, they come to England. At school, Sumitra mixes with children of different backgrounds and cultures, and is encouraged to be free-thinking and independent. She rebels against the idea of an arranged marriage and a style of life decided for her by her parents, who are strict Hindus. Like many immigrants to Britain, Sumitra has to make a choice about how she will live and the kind of future that's possible for her. And her difficulties are not made any easier by the fact that she is a woman in a country still dominated by men.

Sumitra's Story by Rukshana Smith

B

> When Fran's mother first took her to visit old Tom Treloar, Fran had no idea how close she would become to this old man, his home and his past. He opens up new interests and pastimes for her, and when he tells her about the seal cave, Fran enlists the help of Dave in a search for the carved fox-and-geese pieces that Tom Treloar had found and left behind so long ago. The story is a love story, of a teenage girl's awakening to awareness of adult emotions . . . The contrast between the stark reality of the hospital world and the wild beauty of a hidden Cornish valley is yet another delight. In John Branfield's sympathetic hands the positive and life-enhancing aspects of a relationship between young and old are convincingly portrayed.

The Fox in Winter by John Branfield

C

> Set at the dawn of history, this is the tale of Crookleg, a boy who wanted to become not a hunter or a warrior but an artist. Treece's language is simple, but behind the apparent simplicity are greater depths: the book is really concerned with the power and vulnerability of the artist in society.

The Dream-Time by Henry Treece

Now look at the novel you are presently reading. Does it have a blurb?

If so, can you distinguish between the elements of story

and theme? If not, write a suitable blurb to include these elements.

What I meant was . . . !

Let's look now at two methods used by the writer to convey his idea or theme.

The first of these is the **explicit statement**.

Here the writer actually says in so many words what he's getting at. He can do this in a very straightforward manner by speaking in his own voice, breaking into the flow of the story to make a direct comment.

John Steinbeck uses this technique in *The Pearl*. Here are some examples:

'. . . there is no need for speech if it is only a habit anyway.'

'. . . there is no alms-giver in the world like a poor man who is suddenly lucky.'

'. . . every man in the world functions to the best of his ability, and no one does less than his best, no matter what he may think about it.'

'To determine to go and to say it was to be halfway there.'

And finally:

> 'A town is a thing like a colonial animal. A town has a nervous system and a head and shoulders and feet. A town is a thing separate from all other towns, so that there are no two towns alike. And a town has a whole emotion. How news travels through a town is a mystery not easily to be solved. News seems to move faster than small boys can scramble and dart to tell it, faster than women can call it over the fences . . .

From *The Pearl* by John Steinbeck

Not only is Steinbeck using his own voice to talk about one particular town, La Paz; he is using it to convey his idea of towns in general.

Another way of using the technique of explicit statement is to have one of the characters say or think what is on the author's mind.

In Rukshana Smith's novel, *Sumitra's Story*, the heroine has to make a choice about how she will live and the kind of future that's possible for her in her adopted country.

The writer's ideas are conveyed to us through what Sumitra *says* and *thinks*.

 Says

 Thinks

'Yes, yes!' Sumitra cried excitedly . . .

'That's just it . . . It means doing something because it's always been done, even if you think it's wrong, because not continuing the tradition will cause too much trouble. So you get a long line of conformists doing what is expected of them. That's fair enough when the expectations are reasonable and rational, but when they lead to fear and isolation and hatred and . . .' her voice broke and she sat down.

Sumitra thought about this as she chewed a blade of grass. At school she had seen representatives of various groups, Jews, Greeks, Turks, Arabs, Chinese, West Indians, Irish all happily playing together and conforming to the larger ideal of the school community, but going home to continue living in the ways of their parents. They went off to Jewish/ Greek/Turkish/Irish youth clubs so that they would marry Jewish/Greek/ Turkish/Irish partners and bring up Jewish/Greek/Turkish/Irish children. What was it all for? Why couldn't they all mix with whom they liked and bring their children up as human beings living in a country called England?

From *Sumitra's Story* by Rukshana Smith

Activity Does your own book contain examples of explicit statements? If so, choose two or three that you find particularly interesting, and for each of them say whether the author is speaking direct or through one of his characters.

The second method used by a writer to convey his theme is that of the **implicit statement**.

Here the author will *suggest* something rather than state it directly. It is then up to the reader to derive an understanding of what the author is trying to say.

To give a simple example: instead of saying 'He was frightened', an author will suggest that the character was frightened by describing how he looked or what he did.

In *A Kestrel for a Knave*, Barry Hines wants to convey certain things about the games master, Mr Sugden. He does this by implying or suggesting various aspects of his character, as these examples illustrate:

A

He was wearing a violet tracksuit. The top was embellished with cloth badges depicting numerous crests and qualifications, and on the breast a white athlete carried the Olympic torch. The legs were tucked into new white football socks, neatly folded at his ankles, and his football boots were polished as black and shiny as the bombs used by assassins in comic strips. The laces binding them had been scrubbed white, and both boots had been fastened identically: two loops of the foot and one of the ankle, and tied in a neat bow under the tab at the back.

B

   'Tibbut, come out here and be the other captain.'
   Tibbut walked out and stood facing the line, away from Mr Sugden.
   'I'll have first pick, Tibbut.'
   'That's not right, Sir.'
   'Why isn't it?'
   ''Cos you'll get all the best players.'
   'Rubbish, lad.'
   'Course you will, Sir. It's not fair.'
   'Tibbut. Do you want to play football? Or do you want to get dressed and go and do some maths?'
   'Play football, Sir.'
   'Right then, stop moaning and start picking. I'll have Anderson.'

C

'. . . Mr Sugden jogged to the sideline, dropped the ball, and took off his tracksuit. Underneath he was wearing a crisp red football shirt with white cuffs and a white band round the neck. A big white 9 filled most of the back, whiter than his white nylon shorts, which showed a slight fleshy tint through the material. He pulled his socks up, straightened the ribs, then took a fresh roll of half inch bandage from his tracksuit and ripped off two lengths . . . Mr Sugden used the lengths of bandage to secure his stockings just below the knees, then he folded his tracksuit neatly on the ground, looked down at himself, and walked on to the pitch carrying the ball like a plum pudding on the tray of his hand.

From *A Kestrel for a Knave* by Barry Hines

Even from these brief extracts you are probably able to derive certain aspects of Mr Sugden's character, not because of what the author has said directly but because of what he has implied. Now write down what you think Barry Hines is suggesting about Mr Sugden.

Activity   Does your own book contain examples of implicit statements? If so, choose two or three that you find particularly interesting; say why you have chosen them, what ideas they convey, and how successful they are.

We hope that you are now more able to recognise the various ideas and themes that appear in the books you read. Being able to do so will help you towards a more intelligent, and therefore more enjoyable, reading of a given novel.
    Remember what John Bowden said in the earlier interview:

> '. . . a good novel does more than just entertain. From the reader's point of view, it should open a door to his understanding – make him more aware of the world than he was before.'

Activity   You should now be in a better position to agree or disagree with what John Bowden says here.
    How true is it as far as your own reading is concerned?
    Discuss what he says with other members in your group. How many instances of increased awareness or understanding can you recall? What books were involved? To what extent do the themes of these books mirror your own experiences in life?

7 *Style I*

'All styles are good, except the boring ones.' (Voltaire)

Question: How do you make a cigarette lighter?
Answer: Take the tobacco out!

Questions: What has four legs and flies?
Answer: A dead horse!

It's not what you say, it's the way that you say it!

You are much too intelligent to get caught by riddles like these, of course, but if you were confused for a moment, don't worry.

Words can play tricks on you, as the writer Laurie Lee discovered one day.

In this extract from *Cider with Rosie*, Laurie returns home from his first day at school:

> 'What's the matter, Loll? Didn't he like it at school then?'
> 'They never gave me the present!'
> 'Present? What present?'
> 'They said they'd give me a present.'
> 'Well, now, I'm sure they didn't.'
> 'They did! They said: "You're Laurie Lee, ain't you? Well, just you sit there for the present." I sat there all day but I never got it. I ain't going back there again!'

From *Cider with Rosie* by Laurie Lee

Activity   There are many words that can lead to misunderstandings like this. The word 'ruler', for example, can refer to someone who rules, like a king, or to a straight piece of plastic used for measuring.

How many other words like this can you find?

Put the kettle on, please dear

When we are talking, we often use words in a sloppy or imprecise way, but what we say makes sense because we co-operate with each other. So if we are asked, 'What's on the television?' we are more likely to reply, 'The six o'clock news' than give the answer, 'A vase of flowers.'

Activity

We also have different ways of talking.

Discuss the different ways you speak to your parents, to your teachers and to your friends.

Styles of writing

Just as we have different ways of talking, so we all have different styles of writing.

Activity

To what type of reader might the sentences below have been written, and in what circumstances? Pick out words and phrases that give you a clue to the identity of the reader.

Sentences	Reader and situation	Clue words
1 Hi folks! Arrived safely. Weather great! Wish you were here.		
2 I must inform you that a repetition of such appalling service will result in my taking my custom elsewhere.		
3 I hope this information will help you to consider my application favourably.		
4 Two extra pints today, please.		

5 I hope you're behaving yourself for mummy, and doing lots of little jobs around the house.

6 I was patrolling the area of the Albert Street flats when I noticed the vehicle in question parked on a grass verge.

7 Apologies, darling. Had to dash off to Mother's. Dinner in the oven. Love.

8 I want to see an improvement in your next piece of homework.

Danger! Words at work

Because words can cause confusion if used in an imprecise way, novelists have to be particularly careful when using them. When an author sits down to write a novel, he has approximately half a million words to choose from. He also has several ways or techniques of using these words to achieve the emphasis or arrangement he wants. It is the way in which the writer uses these different techniques that will determine what we call his style.

You are now either: (a) totally confused, or: (b) confident that you know a great deal about style.

Confused?
Try to think of it in terms of articles of clothing.

Two boys are each given identical articles: a coat, jumper, shirt, a pair of trousers, socks, shoes and a hat.

Now look at the way each boy uses the clothes.

The point is that while the articles of clothing (the WHAT) are the same, the boys use them in different ways (the HOW).

The way in which each boy has used the clothes is what we might call his style.

Confident?
Just as no two people are exactly alike, so no two people will use their native language in exactly the same way.

Each writer has a personal way of choosing and arranging the words and techniques available to him. It has even been claimed that one writer's work can be distinguished from another's by using a computer. Can you imagine how busy such a computer is likely to be?

Activity   Working in small groups, discuss the different 'styles' of dress that you are familiar with both at home and in school.

Style is how you write a thing

When a writer sits down at his desk, he has thousands of words he can use, plus a few techniques as to how to use them.

He thinks of three things: WHAT he is going to write about (subject), WHY he is going to write about it (purpose), WHO he is writing it for (audience).

When he has made up his mind about these three things, he decides which words to use and how to use them.

Whether he makes a good job of it will depend on how well he can control all the different words and make them do what he wants.

It might sound easy, but words can be tricky little things. You've got to show them who's in charge, just as Humpty Dumpty did in Lewis Carroll's book, *Through the Looking Glass*.

'The question is,' said Alice, 'whether you *can* make words mean so many different things.'

'The question is,' said Humpty Dumpty, 'which is to be Master – that's all.'

Alice was too much puzzled to say anything, so after a minute Humpty Dumpty began again.

'They've got a temper, some of them – particularly verbs, they're the proudest – adjectives you can do anything with, but not verbs – however, I can manage the whole lot of them! . . .'

'When I make a word to do a lot of work . . . ,' said Humpty Dumpty, 'I always pay it extra.'

'Oh!' said Alice. She was too much puzzled to make any other remark.

'Ah, you should see 'em come round me of a Saturday night,' Humpty Dumpty went on, wagging his head gravely from side to side: 'for to get their wages, you know.'

From *Through the Looking Glass* by Lewis Carroll

Style is . . .

abstract	forceful	rich
abusive	graceful	sarcastic
anecdotal	grandiose	satirical
animated	humorous	simple
biblical	impressionistic	stately
concrete	intense	surrealistic
contemptuous	ironical	terse
conversational	lively	unadorned
delicate	lyrical	verbose
dignified	persuasive	whimsical
dramatic	plain	wordy
flowery	realistic	

Activities

1 Look carefully at the list of words just given. How many do you understand? How many could you use in a sentence? Working with a partner, look up the words you don't understand and write a sentence or two to illustrate their meaning.

2 Consider the book you are reading at the moment. Write down all the words in the list above that could be used to describe your novel.

Words in action

Before we go any further, let us look at how some novelists have used words to deal with a subject: in these extracts they are writing about parents and children.

A

> All of a sudden Joby was afraid . . . for the first time, he'd learned they were going to cut his mother open. He hadn't realised it was anything as bad as that. For the first time there leaped into his mind the possibility that she wouldn't come back. His mouthful of sausage tasted like a wad of stale bread.
>
> 'I don't want you to go,' he said. He was crying now, helplessly . . .
>
> 'Don't go, Mam,' he said. 'Don't go.'
>
> She was over by his side, pressing his face into the soft stuff of her frock and stroking his hair.
>
> 'There, there. Come on now, Joby. Where's my big brave lad? I've got to go, lad, because if I don't they can't make me better, can they? And the sooner I go the quicker I'll be home again. There's nothing to worry about. Nothing at all. I'll be back again, all done and dusted, before you hardly know I've been away.'
>
> She handed him her own small square of handkerchief.
>
> 'Come on, now, dry your eyes.'

From *Joby* by Stan Barstow

Activity

What sort of person is Joby's mother? How would you describe the relationship between Joby and his mother? Select words and phrases to support your answers.

B

> Mrs Casper turned her shoes over in her hands, licking her fingers and trying to erase the scuff marks on the heels, then she breathed all over them and rubbed them up on the edge of the tablecloth.
>
> 'These could have done with a polish. Still, ne'er mind, it'll soon be dark.'
>
> She stepped into them and looked round at the backs of her legs.
>
> 'There's no ladders in these stockings, is there, Billy?'
>
> Billy looked at her legs and shook his head.
>
> 'I can't see any.'
>
> 'That's summat anyway. What you going to do wi' yourself tonight, love?'
>
> 'Read my book.'
>
> 'That's nice. What's it about?'
>
> 'Falconry. I'm goin' to get a young Kestrel an' train it.'
>
> 'A Kestrel, what's that?'
>
> 'A Kestrel hawk, what do you think it is?'
>
> 'I say, what time is it?'
>
> 'I've cleaned t'bottom shed out ready, an' I've built a little nesting box out of an orange box 'til . . .'
>
> 'Ten to eight! Ee, I'm goin' to be late as usual.'
>
> She ran into the hall and started to search through a heap of clothes draped over the bannister, peeling them off and throwing them down until she came to her coat.
>
> 'Here, there's two bob for you. Go and buy yourself some pop an' some crisps or summat.'
>
> She slid the florin on to the mantelpiece and smiled at herself through the mirror.
>
> 'And don't be still up when I come in.'

From *A Kestrel for a Knave* by Barry Hines

Activity   What is your impression of Mrs Casper as a mother? What is her attitude towards her son, Billy?

Support your answers with evidence from the passage.

Finally, here is a passage dealing with a father and his son.

C

> Conrad rattled the handle of the toilet.
>
> His Dad was in there. His Dad spent half his time in there.
>
> His Dad was supposed to be a writer but as far as Conrad could see, he spent half his time in the toilet, and the other half sitting about staring as if he'd just been knocked out.
>
> 'Dad!'

'DAD!!'
'What?'
'WHEN ARE YOU COMING OUT???'
'How should I know?'
'Four letters,' said Conrad. 'Three bills and a letter from the BBC to say your plays are no good.' Silence from the bog. Conrad pushed the BBC one under the door.
'Says you're the worst writer in the world. Says don't send us any more plays till you can learn to write good ones.'
More silence from the toilet.
'Are you *deaf*?'
'DAD!'
. . . .Conrad went down to breakfast. He knew that when his Dad came out, the pong on the landing would be lethal to boys.

From *Conrad's War* by Andrew Davies

Activity

What is Conrad's attitude towards his father? How would you describe their relationship?

Try to explain the reasoning behind your answers to these questions.

Style and subject

All of the extracts above deal more or less with the same subject.

What is this subject?

Which of the parents and children did you particularly like or dislike? Can you explain what you liked or disliked about them?

Your answers to the last two questions are very important.

You see, you've been led to form opinions about people you've never met. Take extract B, for example: you probably don't like Mrs Casper very much and you sympathise with Billy.

Can you explain why?

What you must realise is that the writer – in this case Barry Hines – uses certain words and techniques to make you feel this way about his characters.

Your reaction is the effect he was looking for. If he has been successful in obtaining this reaction, it is because he has used an appropriate (i.e. effective) style.

You see, it isn't possible to separate a writer's style from his subject.

It's just my style!

All of the writers here have used words and ways of combining words to create atmosphere, convey mood, arouse emotions, describe places, create characters, convey dialogue, and so on.

In each case, it is the sum total of *how* they have done all these things that we are concerned with when we talk about STYLE.

Remember this when you read through the following extracts. In each case, consider what effect the writer is trying to achieve and how he goes about his task.

D

> Between Saffron Hill and Turnmill Street stood – or, rather slouched, the Red Lion Tavern. A very evil-looking, tumble-down structure, weather-boarded on three sides and bounded on the fourth by the great Fleet Ditch, which stank and gurgled and gurgled and stank by day and night, like the parlour of the Tavern itself.

From *Smith* by Leon Garfield

Activity

The young hero of the book lives here. Would you like to do so? Why not? How has the writer made you react in this way?

Discuss your answers with a partner.

E

> . . . There was an apple tree, ancient and gnarled, . . . and not far from it a well, its windlass a part of its circular brick wall just visible above a profusion of nettles. Then fragments of an old garden fence poking up above the greenery and still managing to confine a riot of deep mauve and vermilion where lilacs and rhododendrons ran amok and threatened to pour out into the meadow.
>
> But at the heart of it all lay the supreme wonder: a two-storeyed red brick house with a lean-to at one side, a quarter of its tiled roof gone, as though untidily pecked out by some gigantic bird! A house, solitary and uninhabited, with cobweb-bed windows, cracked or glassless, and a front door that tapped in the breeze like a thoughtful finger. A secret, unexpected house whose existence had never been dreamed of by Elvira.

From *Summer of the Zeppelin* by Elsie McCutcheon

Activity Would you like to know more about the strange old house? Why? Is it because there is something mysterious about the place? Is this the effect the writer has been seeking in this passage?

How well has she succeeded? More importantly, can you explain *how* she has succeeded?

Here is one more example before we move on to examine some of the writer's techniques in more detail.

F

> 'It may be only blackmail,' said the man in the taxi hopefully. The fog was like a saffron blanket soaked in ice water. It had hung over London all day and at last was beginning to descend. The sky was yellow as a duster and the rest was a granular black overprinted in grey and lightened by occasional slivers of bright fish colour as a policeman turned in his wet cape.
>
> Already the traffic was at an irritable crawl. By dusk it would be stationary. To the west the park dripped wretchedly and to the north the great railway terminus slammed and banged and exploded hollowly about its affairs. Between lay winding miles of butter-coloured stucco in every conceivable state of repair. The fog had crept into the taxi where it crouched panting in a traffic jam. It oozed in ungenially, to smear sooty fingers over the two elegant young people who sat inside.

From *Tiger in the Smoke* by Margery Allingham

In this extract, there is a clever blend of colour and noise and movement which combine to give a very depressing and rather sinister impression of London fog. Put this together with the remark about blackmail and the book's mysterious title, and we begin to imagine the worst for the young people sitting in the taxi.

The overall effect is to make us want to read further and see what happens next.

In the next chapter we will examine more closely some of the techniques of style used by writers to achieve effects of this kind.

8 *Style II*

How's it done?

A writer wants you to understand and enjoy what he has written, and these are some of the techniques he will use to achieve these aims:

diction   imagery   sentence variety   tone

When you are discussing a novelist's style, you will need:
- to recognise these techniques
- to point them out
- to say how they help you appreciate what the writer is trying to say.

Diction

To study a writer's diction is to study his choice of words. If a writer chooses the wrong words, the effect he wants to create, the responses he wants to set up in your mind, will be destroyed.

If you are commenting on a passage from a novel, it is not enough to write: 'This passage is very exciting.' You must find reasons why it is exciting. You need to consider these questions:

1 Why has the writer chosen these words on this occasion?

2 What is the effect of these words?

A writer will choose a certain word or combination of words because:
- it has the exact meaning required
- it has particular associations
- it has the appropriate sound or rhythm
- it conveys a character
- it describes an event or situation
- it contains exactly the right image for his purpose.

The most important of these is probably the word's associations.

Look at the words 'clever' and 'cunning'. They both refer to 'intelligence', yet 'clever' suggests the constructive quality of a skill or talent, while 'cunning' suggests the more destructive quality of deceit.

Here is an example of what we mean:

The police questioned the group of youths.
The police interrogated the gang of teenagers.

Activities

1 Make up twenty sentences of your own. Ten sentences should be favourable and ten should be unfavourable.

2 Complete the following table by choosing the right word from Column 4 to create a favourable or unfavourable impression. The first one is done for you.

Column 1	Column 2	Column 3	Column 4
Favourable	Word	Unfavourable	Word choice
stout	overweight stubborn slim guerrilla chatter careful punish known work old	fat	stout, fat pig-headed, firm skinny, slender freedom fighter, terrorist talk, gossip fussy, particular discipline, victimise notorious, famous chore, career senile, venerable

3 Select one of the passages quoted in the previous chapter, and:
  (a) make a list of any 'favourable' or 'unfavourable' words used by the author;
  (b) comment on the writer's choice of words.

4 Now do the same with a passage selected from the novel you are reading at the moment.

Imagery

Just as a writer will use certain words because of their associations, so he will use certain techniques to call up pictures in your mind.

He will be trying to make you think in a particular way.

When he uses a word or words in this way, we say he is using imagery. The importance of imagery is that it can suggest atmosphere or meaning without the author having to be explicit.

An image, then, is a picture or impression in the mind created by words.

Certain figures of speech are used to help create these pictures. Three of the most popular figures of speech used by writers are similes, metaphors, and personification.

Simile

A simile is a figure of speech in which two things are compared in order to achieve a striking descriptive effect. The comparison is usually introduced by 'like' or 'as'.

Look at these examples:

The fog was like a saffron blanket soaked in ice-water.

The sky was yellow as a duster.

. . . a front door that tapped in the breeze like a thoughtful finger.

In the first example, we get an idea or picture of the colour and freezing-cold nature of the fog which covers or 'blankets' everything and everybody.

Activities

1 How effective do you think the other two examples of simile are? Do they create pictures in your imagination?

2 Now look at the extracts quoted in the previous chapter. Make a list of all the similes you can find and comment on their effectiveness.

3 Select an extract from the novel you are reading at the moment. Copy down any similes contained in the passage and comment on their effectiveness.

Metaphor

A writer can make a striking comparison between different things by saying that something *is* something else.

Look at this example:

> Nothing moved over the landscape except a thin worm of smoke from a distant engine.

The writer does not say that the smoke was *like* a thin worm. He goes further: he says that, for him, the smoke *is* a thin worm. This is a metaphor.

Here is another example:

> The spider patiently spread its net across the void.

The spider does not really spread nets, but the writer has, for the moment, turned him into someone who does, i.e. a fisherman. This, then, is a metaphor. 'Spread its net' is a metaphor for a spider making its web.

Activities

1 Now you know what a metaphor is, look again at the extracts given in the previous chapter. Make a list of any metaphors you can find and discuss their effectiveness with a partner.

2 Select a passage or chapter from the novel you are reading at the moment and copy down all the metaphors it contains. Remember to say whether you find them effective or not and to give reasons for your answers.

Personification

A personification is simply a metaphor which suggests that the object or thing is alive and has human qualities. Here are some examples:

> The fog had crept into the taxi where it crouched panting . . .
> The breakfast table waited impatiently for the first visitors to arrive.

> Blazing and crackling, the fire raced through the forest
> devouring everything in its path.

The fog, table and fire have taken on human qualities. This is personification.

Activities

1 Look back over the extracts quoted in the previous chapter. Copy down any examples of personification you find; in each case explain the significance of the personification, and say whether you find it effective or not.

2 Select an extract from the novel you are reading at the moment. Copy down any examples of personification contained in the passage and comment on their effectiveness.

Remember

It is not enough to be able to recognise examples of figures of speech in a writer's work.

The important thing is not to say 'this is an image', but 'the author uses imagery effectively when he says this because it suggests . . . which is what the writer needs and wants to suggest.'

Activity

The following extract, from Leon Garfield's novel *Smith*, contains several examples of different types of imagery. Make a list of all the ones you can find and comment on their effectiveness. Then compare your list with that of your partner.

Now he was in High Holborn, and the tall buildings on either side scowled blackly down with, here and there through an ill-lit drawn drape, a yellow sneer of light; while ceaselessly down the wide street, like the Devil's own crossings' sweeper, came a bitter wind, whipping up the Town's rubbish into spiteful ghosts of dust and paper that plucked and nipped and stung the living boy.

His nose, chin and fingers were beginning to burn with the cold. Not a night to be out in: black and windy, with the moon now doused in a creeping sea of cloud. He passed by a gloomy ale-house with a bunch of iron grapes groaning from its sign. He stopped – fingered a guinea he'd got with the handkerchief – and thought of a bed for the night. But the house was full, so he took a half pint of gin to keep out the cold, the loneliness and the shifting fear – to no purpose . . .

> Out again into the bitter street. Above his head the iron grapes creaked menacingly, back and forth – back and forth . . .
>
> He moved away, fearful that they'd drop and crack him like an egg.
>
> But it was not the grapes above; the very houses seemed to be shuddering against the blotched sky. He shifted out into the middle of the street, for he'd a sudden horror that all the buildings were tottering in upon him. The sky seemed to grow smaller and smaller and the jagged roofs, fanged with chimneys, seemed to snarl and snap as if to gobble him up. He began to run, wildly: now from side to side of the street, banging into posts, stumbling across the gutter, turning down lanes and alleys that were new even to him . . . And all this with a curious, hopeless urgency: his feet running like a hanged man's feet – seeming to reach for a purchase on a world that was slipping away.

From *Smith* by Leon Garfield

Sentence variety

Consider the use of variety in sentence length in the following example:

> Stuart had made up his mind. He would try to see Amber. It would be difficult, and more than once he told himself he was making a great mistake. The journey didn't help. The bus crawled from stop to stop, and at every one there was an interminable delay as more and more Saturday night revellers searched for the correct change or engaged the driver in idle banter. After what seemed an age, Stuart alighted – Hill Road, and a minute's brisk walk found him standing in front of Amber's house. He paused at the entrance. Then, taking a deep breath, he pushed open the gate, strode purposefully up the gravelled pathway, and rapped loudly on the panelled door.

Notice the length of the first two sentences – just six words in each. The impact is strong. The next sentence is of medium length, giving the writer room to express the tension experienced by the main character. Another carefully controlled short sentence follows, further increasing the tension. Two longer sentences are added, basically describing the events of the journey, and at the same time reflecting Stuart's growing sense of impatience. The final sentences suggest the new-found resolution of the main character.

This feature of varied sentence length plays an important part in the effectiveness of the paragraph, both by keeping the writing lively and by helping to create a mood.

Activity

Think about the novel you are reading at the moment. Have you noticed the actual variety of sentence length? Choose a passage from the book and analyse the sentence length.

Writers also make use of different sentence forms: the **periodic sentence** and the **loose sentence** are two examples.

The periodic sentence

This is designed to hold you in suspense by keeping the important sense until the end. For example:

> As long as the outside culture remained beyond their house, Amber's father was content.

The advantage of the periodic sentence to the writer is that it stimulates the reader's interest. It makes the reader want to know what happens in the sentence and encourages him to read on.

The loose sentence

This is a much more common form. It gives the main sense at the beginning, and does not use the element of delay to hold a reader in suspense. For example:

> Amber's father was content, as long as the outside culture remained beyond their house.

The sentence now could end after 'content' and would be accepted by the reader.

Here is another example:

> Amber was pleased to see him, although she worried what her parents would think.

The loose sentence is very popular with modern authors because it is suited to a plain, straightforward style of writing.

Activities

1 Look at the novel you are reading at the moment and make a list of five periodic sentences.

2 Make a list of ten periodic sentences that relate to some aspect of the novel you are reading at the moment. They may be about plot, character, setting, background, beginnings, endings or a combination of elements.

3 Examine the novel you are reading at the moment and make a list of five loose sentences.

4 Make a list of ten loose sentences that relate to the novel you are reading at the moment. As with the periodic sentences, choose any aspect of the novel you wish.

Remember
- The form of a sentence does not affect its length.
- Loose and periodic sentences can be either long or short.
- Short sentences are particularly useful when a writer wants to be forceful and clear, and when he wants to reinforce the speed of events.
- Longer sentences are more frequently used when he wants to express complicated thoughts and needs space to develop an idea, or when he wants to give the impression that events are happening in a rather leisurely way.
- In general, a good style mixes short, medium and long sentences, and combines the periodic with the loose.

Activity Select a representative passage from the novel you are reading, and comment on the sentence structure. Discuss your comments with a partner.

Tone

Read this sentence to yourself:

I am going to see her tonight.

It looks a straightforward statement, doesn't it? But try saying it aloud again, each time emphasising the words underlined:

1 <u>I am</u> going to see her tonight.
2 I am going to see her <u>tonight</u>.
3 I am going to <u>see</u> her <u>tonight</u>.

You see, a simple statement like this can be interpreted in several different ways depending on the tone in which it is made.

In spoken language, the tone can reveal emotion such as sympathy or anger depending on whether the words are uttered gently and kindly, or sharply and abruptly. In other words, the correct emphasis can be conveyed by the voice.

But in literature there is no audible voice to communicate tone. A writer must use other devices to convey an attitude.

By now, we hope you should be able to recognise some of these devices: word choice, imagery, and sentence structure. All of these must be considered when commenting on the tone of a piece of writing.

When you are writing about tone, you are referring to a writer's attitude to his subject and audience.

The following words are generally used to describe various tones:

calm	earnest	personal
condescending	excited	philosophical
cynical	good-humoured	sarcastic
detached	impersonal	savage
dogmatic	intimate	serious
dramatic	mocking	solemn

Activities

1 Look back at the various extracts used in the previous chapter. In each case:
(a) comment on the tone of the passage, and
(b) examine the techniques used by the writer to convey tone.

2 Select one or more extracts from the novel you are reading at the moment; comment on the tone and the techniques used to convey it.

3 Look again at the list of words that are generally used to describe tone. Can you think of any more?

4 Examine the novel you are reading at the moment. Which of the words in the list relate to your book? Does the 'tone' of the novel change as the plot progresses? Why do you think this is so?

Comprehension
1 When a writer sits down to begin writing, he asks himself three questions. What are they?

2 Choose five words to describe different styles of writing. Write down five sentences to demonstrate these styles.

3 Give a single word which means 'choice of words'.

4 Explain why writers choose their words very carefully.

5 Why is the use of imagery important to a writer?

6 Explain in your own words the difference between a simile and a metaphor.

7 Why will a good writer vary the length of his sentences?

8 Explain in your own words the difference between a loose sentence and a periodic sentence.

9 Choose five words to describe different tones in writing. Write down five sentences to demonstrate these tones.

10 Explain in your own words what you understand by the phrase 'a writer's style'.

Checklist

We hope the following checklist will help you in your revision of the points covered in these two chapters:

Question
Comment on the characteristics of the author's style as seen in . . .

Checklist:
(a) Comment on the diction or word choice: explain why you think certain words have been chosen and what effect they have.
(b) Comment on the imagery: explain what atmosphere or meaning is suggested by the use of figures of speech; give specific examples and comment on their effectiveness.
(c) Comment on the sentence structure and variety: look for particular forms and lengths and explain why they have been used and how effective they are.
(d) Comment on the tone of the writing: indicate which tone or tones appear in the work and explain how they reflect the writer's attitude to his subject and audience.

Extended activities
1 Comment on the characteristics of the author's style as shown in the novel you are reading at the moment.

2 Find two passages, each written by a different author but dealing with a similar subject, and comment on the respective styles of the writers concerned.

3 Collect and comment on examples of different styles of writing from various newspapers (e.g. two articles describing a football match or a court case).

4 Write two versions of the opening paragraphs of a novel, using the first person and then the third.

Briefly explain which method of writing you found the more enjoyable, and why.

5 Think carefully about the styles of writing used in certain types of fiction, e.g. westerns or romances. Go to your local library and find examples of different types of novels. Copy out one passage from each example. Working with a partner, exchange your passages and see if you can recognise the 'style'.

6 Choose an event from the book you are reading at the moment and write two descriptions of that event – one in the style of a 'scandal' paper and one in the style of a 'quality' paper.

7 Think about your school assembly. Is it taken by different people? Does the 'style' of the assembly depend on the person conducting it?

Now, imagine that you have to take the next assembly. Write down exactly how you would organise the event, including what you would say. Show your work to a partner and ask him or her to analyse your style.

8 You are organising a fund-raising event for a local charity. Imagine that you are going to address two groups of people of different ages. Write your speech twice, using the appropriate style for each group.

Remember that the basic information must be the same.

9 Book reviews

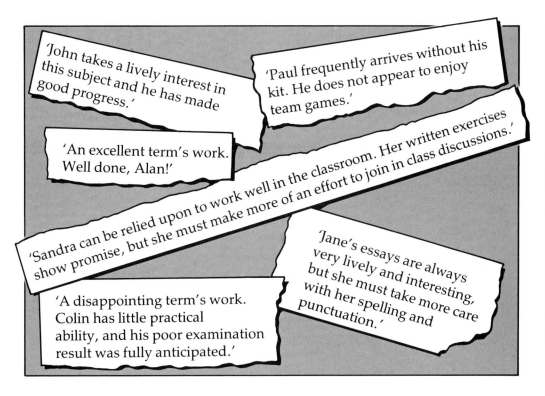

'John takes a lively interest in this subject and he has made good progress.'

'Paul frequently arrives without his kit. He does not appear to enjoy team games.'

'An excellent term's work. Well done, Alan!'

'Sandra can be relied upon to work well in the classroom. Her written exercises show promise, but she must make more of an effort to join in class discussions.'

'Jane's essays are always very lively and interesting, but she must take more care with her spelling and punctuation.'

'A disappointing term's work. Colin has little practical ability, and his poor examination result was fully anticipated.'

SHOCKING REPORT for school pupil!

What did you think of your last school report?

Was it as good or as bad as you expected? Did you agree or disagree with the comments of your teachers? Did you show your report to many people?

Now, think carefully about this question: How would you have felt if your local newspaper had printed your school report?

Pleased? Angry? Shocked? Embarrassed? Shy?

It's an important question because people like novelists or poets or playwrights continually get 'reports' written about them and published in papers and magazines. These reports are called REVIEWS and they are written by CRITICS.

In this chapter, we are going to show you how to write a review; in other words, *you* are going to be writing the report, for a change.

Activities

1 Look through several newspapers and magazines. How many different types of review can you find? Books and films should be fairly obvious, but there are others. Make a list of them and compare your list with that of your partner.

2 Collect all the reviews you can during, say, one week. Arrange them into different subject categories for a classroom display.

3 Ask your teacher how many different types of review are written each year in your school. You will probably be surprised at the answer.

Now look back to the comments at the beginning of the chapter. How many favourable or positive remarks can you find?

There are quite a few, aren't there?

This is an important point because sometimes people think that if they are asked to write a criticism of something, then they can only put unpleasant or negative comments. This is not so.

A critic is a person skilled in judging the merits of something.

We have deliberately left this section until last because all of the previous chapters were designed to give you information gradually and introduce you to various skills that you could eventually put together.

If you have worked carefully through these chapters, CONGRATULATIONS! You can throw away your L-plates and become a critic.

Of course, now that you are a qualified critic, you must expect some criticism yourself:

'Any fool can criticise, and many of them do.'	'Pay no attention to what the critics say; no statue has ever been put up to a critic.'

We really wouldn't want people to say things like that about you, so we've written a checklist for you to follow when criticising or reviewing a book.

Book reviews – the novel

A checklist

Ask yourself these two questions about the book you are reviewing:

1 What is the book about?
2 What do I think of it?

Jot down your answers in note form, and then do the same as you work through these more specific questions and categories.

3 What is the title of the book?
4 Who wrote it and when?
5 What is the subject matter of the book (e.g. detective, history, romance, science fiction, etc.)?
6 What story does the book tell? (Be careful here. Only write a short summary.)
7 What theme(s) does the book deal with? Are the themes stated by the writer, by a character, or are they suggested in some other way?
8 How does the book begin and end? What are my opinions about these sections of the book?
9 Who are the main characters? How do I learn about them? Do they develop and change? Are they flat or rounded?
10 What is the setting for the book? How is it revealed? How important is it?
11 What is the author's style in this book? What is he trying to do? How does he go about it? How successful is he?
12 What do I like about the book?
13 What do I dislike about it?
14 Why would I recommend (or not recommend) it to someone else to read?

Activity   Use the checklist and write a review of a book you have recently read.

Extended activities

1 Write a dialogue in play form between two people who have read the same book but who disagree on its merits.

2 Write as though you are the author of a book. Explain why you wrote it, what effects you were aiming at and how far you consider you have succeeded.

3 Perhaps you have seen a film version or televised serialisation of a book you have read. Write a review of the screen version comparing it to the original.

4 Try to find different reviews – some favourable, some unfavourable – of the same book. What points of similarity and contrast are there in the different reviews?

5 Read a review of a novel you have not read. Explain why you would or would not buy the novel having read the review.

6 Imagine that you are conducting a radio or television interview with the author of a book you have recently read. Script the conversation.

7 Write the script and act out a radio 'phone-in' programme with calls to the author of a book you have recently read.

8 Write a letter to the author of a book, explaining that you have just read his novel, and saying what you think about the book. You could suggest some changes that you believe would improve the book, or perhaps ask for help in understanding certain parts of it.

9 Write the author's letter of reply.

And finally:

10 Write a letter to us explaining what you have liked or disliked about our book. We look forward to hearing from you!